Federal Plain Language Guidelines

Improving Communications

By

Plain Language Action and Information Network

Printed in the United States of America

ISBN: 978-1986407700

Introduction

The Plain Language Action and Information Network (PLAIN) is a community of federal employees dedicated to the idea that citizens deserve clear communications from government. We first developed this document in the mid-90s. We continue to revise it every few years to provide updated advice on clear communication. We hope you find this document useful, and that it helps you improve your writing — and your agency's writing — so your users can:

- find what they need,

- understand what they find; and

- use what they find to meet their needs.

We've divided the document into five major topics, although many of the subtopics fit within more than one topic. We start with a discussion of your audience because you should think about them before you start to write your document or your web content. In fact, you should start to think about them before you start to plan. From there we move to organization, because developing a good organization is important during your planning stage. Next, we discuss writing principles, starting at the word level and moving up through paragraphs and sections. This is the most extensive topic. We follow principles of writing documents with principles of writing for the web. We conclude with a short discussion of testing techniques.

Revision 1 Changes

We have not made any substantive changes in revision 1. We fixed the footer, corrected a few misspelled words, and modified our choice of words to be more concise. We made the formatting more consistent in Section V – Test. We added a few more references to outside publications. And, we changed the file name of this document to make it more descriptive and user-friendly.

Table of Contents

I. Think about your audience

One of the most popular plain language myths is that you have to "dumb down" your content so that everyone everywhere can read it. That's not true. The first rule of plain language is: ***write for your audience***. Use language your audience knows and feels comfortable with. Take your audience's current level of knowledge into account. Don't write for an 8th grade class if your audience is composed of PhD candidates, small business owners, working parents, or immigrants. Only write for 8th graders if your audience is, in fact, an 8th grade class.

Make sure you know who your audience is – don't guess or assume.

a. Identify and write for your audience

You have to grab your audience's attention if you want to get your ideas across. Let's face it, people want to know just what applies to them. The best way to grab and hold someone's attention is to figure out who they are and what they want to know. Put yourself in their shoes; it will give you a new perspective. (Read Identify your users and their top tasks for more information.)

Tell your audience why the material is important to them. Say, "If you want a research grant, here's what you have to do." Or, "If you want to mine federal coal, here's what you should know." Or, "If you are planning a trip to Rwanda, read this first."

Identifying your audience will do more than ensure that you write clearly. It will also help you focus on the audience's needs. Start out by thinking about what your audience knows about the situation now. Then, think about how to guide them from their current knowledge to what you need them to know. To help you do this, try answering the following questions:

- Who is my audience?

- What does my audience already know about the subject?

- What does my audience need to know?

- What questions will my audience have?

- What's the best outcome for my agency? What do I need to say to get this outcome?

- What's the best outcome for our audience? What do I need to say to get this outcome?

Sources
- Garner, Bryan A., *Legal Writing in Plain English*, 2001, University of Chicago Press, Chicago, pp. 93-96.
- Securities and Exchange Commission, *Plain English Handbook*, 1998, Washington, DC, p. 9.

b. Address separate audiences separately

An important part of writing for your audience is addressing separate audiences separately. Many documents address more than one audience. Documents that mix material intended for different audiences may confuse readers. By addressing different audiences in the same place, you make it harder for each audience to find the material that applies to them. In regulations, this may make it difficult for each audience to comply with your agency's requirements.

The following example shows a regulation that treats each regulated group separately in its own subpart, rather than mixing all the groups together in the same subpart. For an example of a rule that does not address separate groups separately, see 5 CFR 1320 (http://ecfr.gpoaccess.gov/cgi/t/text/text-idx?c=ecfr&rgn=div5&view=text&node=5:3.0.2.3.9&idno=5 this link takes a long time to load).

Title 40 — Protection of Environment

Chapter I — Environmental Protection Agency

Part 745 — Lead-Based Paint Poisoning Prevention In Certain Residential Structures

* * *

Subpart E — Residential Property Renovation

(Firms renovating structures)

* * *

745.326   Renovation: State and Tribal program requirements.

745.327   State or Indian Tribal lead-based paint compliance and enforcement programs.

Sources

- Murawski, Thomas A., *Writing Readable Regulations*, 1999, Carolina Academic Press Durham, NC, p. 4.
- Redish, Janice C., *How to Write Regulations and Other Legal Documents in Clear English*, 1991, American Institutes for Research, Washington, DC, p. 17.

II. Organize

Organization is key. Start by stating the document's purpose and its bottom line. Eliminate filler and unnecessary content. Put the most important information at the beginning and include background information (when necessary) toward the end.

a. Organize to meet your readers' needs

People read documents and visit websites to get answers. They want to know how to do something or what happens if they don't do something and they want to gain this knowledge quickly-. Organize your document to respond to these concerns.

Think through the questions your audience is likely to ask and then organize your material in the order they'd ask them. For regulations and other complex documents, create a comprehensive table of contents. Your table of contents should be a reliable road map that users can follow to quickly find the information they need.

Chronological organization

Regulations frequently address processes. Chronological organization is best for process information: you fill out an application to get a benefit; you submit the application; the agency reviews the application; the agency makes a decision on the application. Present the steps chronologically, in the order your user and your agency will follow them. The table of contents below is organized in a logical sequence for a grant program.

Organized chronologically
Part 791–Gifted and Talented Students
Subpart A: How the Grant Program Works
Sec. 791.1 What is the Gifted and Talented Students Education Program? 791.2 Am I eligible for a grant?

General first, exceptions, conditions, and specialized information later

Another useful organizing principle is to put general information first, with specialized information or exceptions to the general information later. That way the material that addresses most readers in most situations comes first. For some documents, this will work well along with a chronological organization. In others, it may be the primary organizing principle.

Here's an example of an administrative regulation that combines both organizing principles:

725.2 What special terms do I need to know to understand this part?

Who is Covered

725.201 Who is entitled to benefits under this program?
725.202 How long can my benefits last?
725.203 Are my dependents entitled to benefits?
725.204 How long will their benefits last?
725.205 Am I still eligible if I am convicted of a felony?

How to Apply for Benefits

725.301 How do I file a claim?
725.302 Can other people give evidence on my behalf?
725.303 Are there any time limits for filing my claim?
725.304 Can I modify or withdraw my claim?

How to Appeal Agency Decisions

725.401 Can I appeal a decision if I don't agree with it?
725.402 How do I file an appeal?
725.403 How long do I have to file an appeal?
725.404 What types of evidence must I submit?
725.405 What happens if I won't get a medical examination?

Limit levels to three or fewer

Crafting documents with four, five, or even more levels makes it difficult for your audience to keep track of where they are in the structure of your document. You should address this problem in your initial structuring of the document. Dividing your document into more pieces at the top levels should allow you to limit subdivisions below the major level to two. The Office of the Federal Register recommends that regulations contain no more than three levels, noting that more than three levels make regulations hard to read and use.

Address separate audiences separately

If you have more than one audience for your document, address each one separately. No one wants to have to wade through material meant for someone else. For more discussion of this issue, see the section Address separate audiences separately.

Sources
- Kimble, Joseph, *Lifting the Fog of Legalese*, 2006, Carolina Academic Press, Durham, NC, p. 70 (C).
- Murawski, Thomas A., *Writing Readable Regulations*, 1999, Carolina Academic Press Durham, NC, pp. 3-5.
- Office of the Federal Register, *Document Drafting Handbook*, 1998, §1-23, www.archives.gov/federal-register/write/handbook/ddh.pdf.
- Redish, Janice C., *How to Write Regulations and Other Legal Documents in Clear English*, 1991, American Institutes for Research, Washington, DC, pp. 12-21.
- Securities and Exchange Commission, *Plain English Handbook*, 1998, Washington, DC, p. 15.

b. Address one person, not a group

Remember that even though your document may affect a thousand or a million people, you are speaking to the one person who is reading it. When your writing reflects this, it's more economical and has a greater impact.

Singular nouns and verbs prevent confusion about whether a requirement applies to individual users or to groups. In the following example, the user might think that each applicant must file applications at several offices.

Confusing plural	Clearer singular
Individuals and organizations wishing to apply must file applications with the appropriate offices in a timely manner.	You must apply at least 30 days before you need the certification. a. If you are an individual, apply at the State office in the State where you reside. b. If you are an organization, apply at the State office in the State where your headquarters is located.

In addressing a single person, you can avoid awkwardness by using "you" to address the user directly, rather than using "he or she" or "his or her."

Confusing plural	Clearer singular
The applicant must provide his or her mailing address and his or her identification number.	You must provide your mailing address and identification number.

Sources

- Garner, Bryan A., *Legal Writing in Plain English*, 2001, University of Chicago Press, Chicago, p. 114.
- Murawski, Thomas A., *Writing Readable Regulations*, 1999, Carolina Academic Press Durham, NC, p. 70.
- Wydick, Richard, *Plain English for Lawyers*, 5th edition, 2005, Carolina Academic Press, Durham, NC, p. 62.

c. Use lots of useful headings

The best-organized document will still be difficult for users to follow if they can't see how it's organized. An effective way to reveal your document's organization is to use lots of useful headings. Headings are also critical for effective web pages (see Writing for the web). You should use headings liberally on the web to help your user accomplish top tasks.

Types of headings

There are three types of headings —

Type of heading	What it is	How it looks
Question Heading	A heading in the form of a question	Why Do We Use Headings?
Statement Heading	A heading that uses a noun and a verb	Headings Help Guide a Reader
Topic Heading	A heading that is a word or short phrase	Headings

Question Headings are the most useful type of heading, but only if you know what questions your audience would ask. Most people come to government documents with questions. If you know those questions, use them as headings. They will help the audience find the information they are looking for quickly. Using the question-and-answer format helps your audience scan the document and find specific information.

Statement Headings are the next best choice because they are still very specific.

Topic Headings are the most formal; many times management is more comfortable with them. But sometimes they're so vague that they just aren't helpful. Topic Headings such as "General," "Application," and "Scope" are so vague they may confuse the user. For example, "Application" might mean an application to your agency from someone reading your document. But it might as easily mean what the document applies to.

Short headings that aren't very helpful to the user	Informative headings capture the user's questions
§ 254.11 Indian Rights.	§254.11 How do the procedures in this part affect Indian rights?
§ 254.12 Applications.	§254.12 How do I apply for a grant under this part?
§ 254.13 Multi-tribal grants.	§254.13. When must I submit my application?
§ 254.14 Administrative requirements.	§254.14 Can a multi-tribal organization submit a single grant request?
§ 254.15 Appeals	§254.15 What special information do I need for an application by a multi-tribal organization?
	§254.16 Must each tribe in a multi-tribal organization submit certification forms and budgets?
	§254.17 If I receive a grant under this part, what requirements must I follow?
	§ 254.18 What reports must I submit after receiving a grant?
	§254.19 How can I appeal administrative actions under this part?

In the example above, the section headings in the right column are more informative than the short topic headings in the left column. Additionally, breaking the material into more sections allows us to capture the entire content of each section in its heading. A document with lots of informative headings is easy to follow because the headings break up the material into logical, understandable pieces.

Use headings to help develop your document's structure

It's often useful to start writing your document by developing the headings, structuring them to your audience's concerns. This approach can also reveal major groupings of information that you might want to identify with centered headings.

Broad topic headings are the first step in organizing the document	Specific topics add the second level of organization
Qualifications of permittees and lessees	Who may hold leases and permits? Can foreign citizens hold permits or leases? How do I file evidence of my qualifications? Can I amend my qualifications statement?
Bonding requirements	Must I file a bond with my permit or lease? Where do I file my bond? What types of bonds are acceptable? How does BLM establish bond amounts? When does BLM terminate my liability under a bond?

Headings can be too long

Headings should not be so long that they overwhelm the material in the section itself. Avoid headings with one-word answers. With rare exceptions, headings should be shorter than the content that follows them.

Heading overwhelms content	Content should be longer than headings
Do I have to file a newspaper notice of my activities before I begin operations? Yes.	**Must I publish a public notice?** You must publish a notice of your operations in a local newspaper before you begin.

Sources

- Garner, Bryan A., *Legal Writing in Plain English*, 2001, University of Chicago Press, Chicago, p. 14-16.
- Kimble, Joseph, *Lifting the Fog of Legalese*, 2006, Carolina Academic Press, Durham, NC, p. 70 (C).
- Murawski, Thomas A., *Writing Readable Regulations*, 1999, Carolina Academic Press Durham, NC, pp. 10-12, 27.
- Office of the Federal Register, *Document Drafting Handbook*, 1998, MMR-2. www.archives.gov/federal-register/write/handbook/.

d. Write short sections

Short sections break up material so it appears easier to comprehend. Long, dense sections with no white space are visually unappealing, and give the impression your document is difficult to understand. Short sections appear easier to comprehend, and help you organize your document more effectively.

Short sections also give you more opportunity to insert informative headings in your material. Remember that boldface section headings give your reader the best roadmap to your document. Long sections are impossible to summarize meaningfully in a heading. When you write short sections, each heading can give the reader information about the entire contents of the section.

Long, dense paragraph	Shorter paragraphs, easier to follow
§ 2653.30 Native group selections. (a) Selections must not exceed the amount recommended by the regional corporation or 320 acres for each Native member of a group, or 7,680 acres for each Native group, whichever is less. Native groups must identify any acreage over that as alternate selections and rank	**§ 2653.31 What are the selection criteria for Native group selections and what lands are available?** You may select only the amount recommended by the regional corporation or 320 acres for each Native member of a group, or 7,680 acres for each Native group, whichever is less. You must

Long, dense paragraph	Shorter paragraphs, easier to follow
their selections. Beyond the reservations in sections 2650.32 and 2650.46 of this Part, conveyances of lands in a National Wildlife Refuge are subject to the provisions of section 22(g) of ANCSA and section 2651.41 of this chapter as though they were conveyances to a village corporation. (b) Selections must be contiguous and the total area selected must be compact except where separated by lands that are unavailable for selection. BLM will not consider the selection compact if it excludes lands available for selection within its exterior boundaries; or an isolated tract of public land of less than 640 acres remains after selection. The lands selected must be in quarter sections where they are available unless exhaustion of the group's entitlement does not allow the selection of a quarter section. The selection must include all available lands in less than quarter sections. Lands selected must conform as nearly as practicable to the United States lands survey system.	identify any acreage over 7,680 as alternate selections and rank their selection. **§ 2653.32 What are the restrictions in conveyances to Native groups?** Beyond the reservations described in this part conveyances of lands in a National Wildlife Refuge are subject to section 22(g) of ANSCA as though they were conveyances to a village. **§ 2653.33 Do Native group selections have to share a border?** Yes, selections must share a border. The total area you select must be compact except where separated by lands that are unavailable for selection. We will not consider your selection if: (a) It excludes lands available for selection within its exterior boundaries; or (b) An isolated tract of public land of less than 640 acres remains after selection. **§ 2653.34 How small a parcel can I select?** Select lands in quarter sections where they are available unless there is not enough left in your group's entitlement to allow this. Your election must include all available lands in areas that are smaller than quarter sections. Conform your selection as much as possible to the United States land survey system.

Sources
- Kimble, Joseph, *Lifting the Fog of Legalese*, 2006, Carolina Academic Press, Durham, NC, pp. 11, 165-174.
- Murawski, Thomas A., *Writing Readable Regulations*, 1999, Carolina Academic Press Durham, NC, pp. 9-10.

III. Write your document

With a relatively small amount of effort and in a relatively short amount of time, you can significantly improve traditionally-written material.

a. Words

Words matter. They are the most basic building blocks of written and spoken communication. Choose your words carefully – be precise and concise.

1. Verbs

Verbs tell your audience what to *do*. Make sure they know *who* does what.

i. Use active voice

Active voice makes it clear who is supposed to do what. It eliminates ambiguity about responsibilities. Not "It must be done., but "You must do it." Passive voice obscures who is responsible for what and is one of the biggest problems with government documents. Don't confuse passive voice with past tense.

In an active sentence, the person or agency that's acting is the subject of the sentence. In a passive sentence, the person or item that is acted upon is the subject of the sentence. Passive sentences often do not identify who is performing the action.

Passive voice	Active voice
The lake was polluted by the company.	The company polluted the lake.
New regulations were proposed.	We proposed new regulations.
The following information must be included in the application for it to be considered complete.	You must include the following information in your application.
Bonds will be withheld in cases of non-	We will withhold your bond if you don't

Passive voice	Active voice
compliance with all permits and conditions.	comply with all permit terms and conditions.
Regulations have been proposed by the Department of Veterans Affairs.	The Department of Veterans Affairs proposed new regulations.
The permit must be approved by the agency's State office.	Our State office must approve your permit.

More than any other writing technique, using active voice and specifying who is performing an action will change the character of your writing.

How do you identify passive sentences?

Passive sentences have two basic features, although both may not appear in every passive sentence.

- A form of the verb "to be" (for example: are, was, were, could be) and

- A past participle (generally with "ed" on the end).

Use passive voice when the law is the actor

In a very few instances, passive voice may be appropriate. For example, when one action follows another as a matter of law, and there is no actor (besides the law itself) for the second action, a passive sentence may be the best method of expression. You might also use passive when it doesn't matter who is doing an action.

For example:

If you do not pay the royalty on your mineral production, your lease will be terminated…

Sources
- Charrow, Veda R., Erhardt, Myra K. and Charrow, Robert P. *Clear & Effective Legal Writing,* 4th edition, 2007, Aspen Publishers, New York, NY, pp. 173-175.
- Garner, Bryan A., *A Dictionary of Modern Legal Usage,* 2nd edition, 1995, Oxford University Press, Oxford and New York, pp. 643-644.
- Garner, Bryan A., *Legal Writing in Plain English,* 2001, University of Chicago Press, Chicago, pp. 24-26.

- Garner, Bryan A., *Garner's Modern American Usage,* 2003. Oxford University Press, Oxford and New York, pp. 892-893.
- Murawski, Thomas A., *Writing Readable Regulations*, 1999, Carolina Academic Press Durham, NC, pp. 73-75.
- Office of the Federal Register, *Document Drafting Handbook*, 1998, p. MMR-5. www.archives.gov/federal-register/write/handbook/ddh.pdf.
- Redish, Janice C., *How to Write Regulations and Other Legal Documents in Clear English,* 1991, American Institutes for Research, Washington, DC, p. 26.
- Securities and Exchange Commission, *Plain English Handbook*, 1998, Washington, DC, pp. 19 –20.

ii. Use the simplest form of a verb

The simplest and strongest form of a verb is present tense. A document written in the present tense is more immediate and less complicated. Using the present tense makes your document more direct and forceful. The more you use conditional or future tense, the harder your audience has to work to understand your meaning. Writing entirely in the present tense saves your audience work and helps make your point clearly.

Don't say	Say
These sections describe types of information that would satisfy the application requirements of Circular A-110 as it would apply to this grant program.	These sections tell you how to meet the requirements of Circular A-110 for this grant program.

Even if you are covering an event that occurred in the past, you can clarify the material for your user by writing as much as possible in the present tense.

Don't say	Say
Applicants who were Federal employees at the time that the injury was sustained should have filed a compensation request at that time. Failure to do so could have an effect on the degree to which the applicant can be covered under this part.	You may not be covered under this part if: a. You were a Federal employee at the time of the injury; and b. You did not file a claim at that time.

Occasionally, of course, you may need to use other tenses. For example, National Environmental Policy Act (NEPA) documents frequently refer to what may happen in the future if certain events occur. But use tenses other than the present only when necessary for accuracy.

iii. Avoid hidden verbs

Use the strongest, most direct form of the verb possible.

Verbs are the fuel of writing. Verbs give your sentences power and direction. They enliven your writing and make it more interesting. Too often, we hide verbs by turning them into nouns, making them less effective and using more words than we need. Hidden verbs are a particular problem in government writing.

What are hidden verbs?

A hidden verb is a verb converted into a noun. It often needs an extra verb to make sense. So we write, "Please make an application for a personal loan" rather than "Please apply for a personal loan."

Hidden verbs come in two forms. Some have endings such as *-ment, -tion, -sion,* and *-ance* or link with verbs such as *achieve, effect, give, have, make, reach,* and *take.* Often, you will find a hidden verb between the words "the" and "of."

Hidden Verb	Uncovered
To trace the missing payment, we need to carry out a review of the Agency's accounts so we can gain an understanding of the reason the error occurred.	To trace the missing payment, we need to review the Agency's accounts so we understand the reason the error occurred.
If you cannot make the payment of the $100 fee, you must make an application in writing before you file your tax return.	If you cannot pay the $100 fee, you must apply in writing before you file your tax return.
This means we must undertake the calculation of new figures for the congressional hearing.	This means we must calculate new figures for the congressional hearing.

Hidden Verb	Uncovered
The production of accurate statistics is important for the committee in the assessment of our homelessness policy.	Producing accurate statistics is important to the committee in assessing our policy on homelessness.

Sources

- Charrow, Veda R., Erhardt, Myra K. and Charrow, Robert P. *Clear & Effective Legal Writing,* 4th edition, 2007, Aspen Publishers, New York, NY, pp. 176-178.
- Garner, Bryan A., *Legal Writing in Plain English*, 2001, University of Chicago Press, Chicago, p. 38 (14.)
- Kimble, Joseph, *Lifting the Fog of Legalese*, 2006, Carolina Academic Press, Durham, NC., p. 71 (D.4).
- Securities and Exchange Commission, *Plain English Handbook,* 1998, Washington, DC., p. 21.
- Wright, Nick, *Hidden Verbs*, at www.plainlanguage.gov/howto/wordsuggestions/hiddenverbs.cfm.

iv. Use "must" to indicate requirements

The word "must" is the clearest way to convey to your audience that they have to do something. "Shall" is one of those officious and obsolete words that has encumbered legal style writing for many years. The message that "shall" sends to the audience is, "this is deadly material." "Shall" is also obsolete. When was the last time you heard it used in everyday speech?

Besides being outdated, "shall" is imprecise. It can indicate either an obligation or a prediction. Dropping "shall" is a major step in making your document more user-friendly. Don't be intimidated by the argument that using "must" will lead to a lawsuit. Many agencies already use the word "must" to convey obligations. The US Courts are eliminating "shall" in favor of "must" in their Rules of Procedure. One example of these rules is cited below.

Instead of using "shall", use:

- "must" for an obligation,
- "must not" for a prohibition,
- "may" for a discretionary action, and
- "should" for a recommendation.

The following example demonstrates how much clearer language can be if you follow these suggestions.

Don't say	Say
Section 5511.1 Free Use of Timber on Oil and Gas Leases a. Any oil or gas lessee who wishes to use timber for fuel in drilling operations shall file an application therefore with the officer who issued the lease. b. The applicant shall be notified by registered mail in all cases where the permit applied for is not granted, and shall be given 30 days within which to appeal such decision. c. Where the land is occupied by a settler, the applicant shall serve notice on the settler by registered mail showing the amount and kind of timber he has applied for.	**Section 5511.1 Free Use of Timber on Oil and Gas Leases** a. You must file an application to use the timber on your oil or gas lease for fuel. File the application with our office where you got your lease. b. We will notify you by registered mail if we reject your application. You must file an appeal of that decision within 30 days. c. You must notify any settler, by registered mail, that you have applied to use timber from your lease. Include in your notice the amount and the kind of timber you intend to use as fuel.

Many legal scholars have written about the problem of "shall." Read a brief summary of several arguments at: www.plainlanguage.gov/howto/wordsuggestions/shallmust.cfm.

Sources

- Charrow, Veda R., Erhardt, Myra K. and Charrow, Robert P. *Clear & Effective Legal Writing,* 4th edition, 2007, Aspen Publishers, New York, NY, pp. 183-184.
- Garner, Bryan A., *A Dictionary of Modern Legal Usage,* 2nd edition, 1995, Oxford University Press, Oxford and New York, pp. 939-942.
- Garner, Bryan A., *Legal Writing in Plain English,* 2001, University of Chicago Press, Chicago, pp. 105-106.
- Kimble, Joseph, *Lifting the Fog of Legalese,* 2006, Carolina Academic Press, Durham, NC, pp. 159-160.
- US Courts, *Federal Rules of Appellate Procedure,* 2009, US Government Printing Office, Washington, DC. www.uscourt.gov/uscourts/rulesandpolicies/rules/ap2009.pdf.
- Wydick, Richard, *Plain English for Lawyers,* 5th edition, 2005, Carolina Academic Press, Durham, NC, p. 64.

v. Use contractions when appropriate

While many legal authorities say that contractions don't belong in legal writing, Bryan Garner, a leading authority on legal writing, advocates their use as a way to make legal writing, including opinions and rules, less stuffy and more natural. Contractions make your writing more accessible to the user. Research shows that that they also enhance readability (DaNielsen and Larosa, 1989).

"Write as you talk" is a common rule of writing readably, and the best way to do that is to use contractions. People are accustomed to hearing contractions in spoken English, and using them in your writing helps people relate to your document.

Use contractions with discretion. Just as you shouldn't bullet everything on a page, you shouldn't make a contraction out of every possible word. Don't use them wherever possible, but wherever they sound natural.

Don't Say	Say
No pilot in command of a civil aircraft may allow any object to be dropped from that aircraft in flight that creates a hazard to persons or property.	If you are a pilot in command of a civil aircraft, don't allow any object that creates a hazard to persons or property to be dropped from that aircraft during flight.

Sources
- DaNielsen , Wayne A. and Dominic L. Larosa, A New Readability Formula Based on the Stylistic Age of Novels, 33 *Journal of Reading* (1989), pp. 194, 196.
- Garner, Bryan A., *Legal Writing in Plain English*, 2001, University of Chicago Press, Chicago, pp. 49-50.
- Garner, Bryan A., *The Elements of Legal Style*, 2002, Oxford Univ. Press, Oxford and New York, pp. 81-82.

2. Nouns and pronouns

Nouns add substance and direction. Pronouns engage your audience. Don't complicate things by using words they won't understand or abbreviations that confuse them.

i. Don't turn verbs into nouns

The bulk of government and technical writing uses too many noun strings – groups of nouns "sandwiched" together. Readability suffers when three words that are ordinarily separate nouns follow in succession. Once you get past three, the string becomes unbearable. Technically, clustering nouns turns all but the last noun into adjectives. However, many users will think they've found the noun when they're still reading adjectives, and will become confused.

Bring these constructions under control by eliminating descriptive words that aren't essential. If you can't do that, open up the construction by using more prepositions and articles to clarify the relationships among the words.

Avoid nouns strings like these	Instead, say
Underground mine worker safety protection procedures development	Developing procedures to protect the safety of workers in underground mines
Draft laboratory animal rights protection regulations	Draft regulations to protect the rights of laboratory animals
National Highway Traffic Safety Administration's automobile seat belt interlock rule	The National Highway Traffic Safety Administration's interlock rule applies to automotive seat belts

Sources

- Charrow, Veda R., Erhardt, Myra K. and Charrow, Robert P. *Clear & Effective Legal Writing,* 4th edition, 2007, Aspen Publishers, New York, NY, pp. 192-193.
- Garner, Bryan A., *A Dictionary of Modern Legal Usage,* 2nd edition, 1995, Oxford University Press, Oxford and New York, pp. 601-602.
- Garner, Bryan A., *Garner's Modern American Usage,* 2003, Oxford University Press, Oxford and New York, p. 557.
- Wydick, Richard, *Plain English for Lawyers,* 5th edition, 2005, Carolina Academic Press, Durham, NC, p. 71.
- Zinsser, William, *On Writing Well,* 6th edition, 2001, HarperCollins, New York, pp. 77-78.

ii. Use pronouns to speak directly to readers

Pronouns help the audience picture themselves in the text and relate better to your documents. More than any other single technique, using "you" pulls users into your document and makes it relevant to them. When you use "you" to address users, they are more likely to understand what their responsibility is. Using "we" to refer to your agency makes your agency more approachable. It also makes your sentences shorter and your document easier to read.

Don't say	Say
Copies of tax returns must be provided.	You must provide copies of your tax returns.

Writing for an individual forces you to analyze carefully what you want the reader to do. By writing to an individual, you will find it easier to:

- Put information in a logical order

- Answer questions and provide the information that your user wants to know

- Assign responsibilities and requirements clearly

Be sure to define "you" clearly.

Don't say	Say
Facilities in regional and district offices are available to the public during normal business hours for requesting copies of agency records.	If you are a private citizen, you can get copies of our records at any regional or district office …

Define "you" by any of the following methods:

- State in the beginning of the document who the user is — "This regulation tells you, the loan applicant, how to secure a loan."

- Define "you" in the Definitions section — "You" means a loan applicant.

- Where you address different users in different parts of the document, define "you" in each context — "How do different types of borrowers apply for a loan? If you are a small business, you must submit … If you are an individual, you must submit …"

It's especially important to define "you" when writing to multiple audiences.

Don't say	Say
Lessees and operators are responsible for restoring the site. You must ensure that …	Lessees and operators are responsible for restoring the site. If you are the lessee, you must monitor the operator to ensure that. If you are the operator, you must conduct all operations in a way …

If you use a question-and-answer format, you should assume that the user is the one asking the questions. Use "I" in the questions to refer to the user. Use "we" in the responses to represent your agency.

Don't say	Say
Submission of applications.	How do I apply?

By using "we" to respond to questions, you state clearly what your agency requires and what your agency's responsibilities are. You also avoid the passive voice and use fewer words. You can define "we" in the definitions sections of your document if that will help the user.

Don't say	Say
Loan applications will be reviewed to ensure that procedures have been followed.	We review your loan application to ensure that you followed our procedures.
The Office of Consumer Affairs will process your application within 30 days after receipt.	We'll process your application within 30 days of receiving it.

Make sure you use pronouns that clearly refer to a specific noun. If a pronoun could refer to more than one person or object in a sentence, repeat the name of the person or object or rewrite the sentence.

Don't say	Say
After the Administrator appoints an Assistant Administrator, he or she must …	After the Administrator appoints an Assistant Administrator, the Assistant Administrator must …

Sources

- Garner, Bryan A., *A Dictionary of Modern Legal Usage*, 2nd edition, 1995, Oxford University Press, Oxford and New York, p. 643.
- Garner, Bryan A., *Legal Writing in Plain English*, 2001, University of Chicago Press, Chicago, p. 50.
- Murawski, Thomas A., *Writing Readable Regulations*, 1999, Carolina Academic Press Durham, NC, pp. 33-38.
- Securities and Exchange Commission, *Plain English Handbook*, 1998, Washington, DC, p. 22.
- Wydick, Richard, *Plain English for Lawyers,* 5th edition, 2005, Carolina Academic Press, Durham, NC.

iii. Minimize abbreviations

One legal scholar calls abbreviations a "menace to prose" (Kimble, 2006). Abbreviations were once intended to serve the audience by shortening long phrases. However, abbreviations have proliferated so much in current government writing that they constantly require the reader to look back to earlier pages, or to consult an appendix, to puzzle out what's being said.

Use "nicknames"

The best solution is to find a simplified name for the entity you want to abbreviate. This gives readers meaningful content that helps them remember what you're talking about. It may be a bit longer, but the gain in clarity and ease of reading is worth it. In most cases, you don't need to "define" this nickname the first time you use it, unless you are using lots of different nicknames. Especially when you are using a nickname for the major topic of your document, don't insult your users and waste their time. For example, in a paper about Resource Advisory Councils, don't tell them that when you say "Council" you mean "Resource Advisory Council."

For	Instead of	Consider
Engineering Safety Advisory Committee	ESAC	the committee
Small-quantity handlers of universal wastes	SQHUW	waste handlers
Fire and Police Employee Relations Act	FPERA	the Act

If everyone knows an abbreviation, use it without explanation

There's a short list of abbreviations that have entered common usage. When you use them, don't define them, you're just taking up space and annoying your user. But make sure the abbreviation you're using is on the list. Examples include IBM, ATM, BMW, PhD, CIA.

A closely related guideline is, "don't define something that's obvious to the user." Most federal agencies, when writing a letter responding to an inquiry, insist on defining the agency name, as in, "Thank you for writing to the Federal Aviation Administration (FAA) about your concerns ..." The letterhead says the name of the agency. The person wrote to the agency, and now the agency is writing back. The user is *not* going to be confused about what FAA means!

If you must abbreviate

Of course, there are some situations in which you can't avoid an abbreviation. Always define an abbreviation the first time you use it, for example, "The American Journal of Plain Language Studies" (AJPLA). And limit the number of abbreviations you use in one document to no more than three, and preferably two. Spell out everything else. If you've used abbreviations for the two or three most common items, it's unlikely that the other items occur so frequently you can't spell them out every time.

When you are considering whether to use an abbreviation, or how many you can get away with in a document, remember that they should make it easier for your users. If they make it harder, you have failed to write for your audience.

Sources
- Garner, Bryan A., *A Dictionary of Modern Legal Usage*, 2nd edition, 1995, Oxford University Press, Oxford and New York, pp. 447-448.
- Garner, Bryan A., *Legal Writing in Plain English*, 2001, University of Chicago Press, Chicago, pp. 46-48.
- Kimble, Joseph, *Lifting the Fog of Legalese*, 2006, Carolina Academic Press, Durham, NC, p. 155.

3. Other word issues

Be concise – leave out unnecessary words. Don't use jargon or technical terms when everyday words have the same meaning. Use words and terms consistently throughout your documents.

i. Use short, simple words

Vocabulary choice is an important part of communicating clearly. While there is no problem with being expressive, most federal writing has no place for literary flair. People do not curl up in front of the fire with a nice federal regulation to have a relaxing read.

Government writing is often stodgy, full of long, dry legalisms and other jargon. Federal government writing is no exception. H.W. Fowler summed up these recommendations for making word choices in his influential book, *The King's English*, first published in 1906. He encouraged writers to be more simple and direct in their style (quoted in Kimble, 2006).

- Prefer the familiar word to the far-fetched.

- Prefer the concrete word to the abstraction.

- Prefer the single word to the circumlocution.

- Prefer the short word to the long.

- Prefer the Saxon word to the Romance word.

Kathy McGinty (www.plainlanguage.gov) offers tongue-in-cheek instructions for bulking up your simple, direct sentences.

> There is no escaping the fact that it is considered very important to note that a number of various available applicable studies ipso facto have generally identified the fact that additional appropriate nocturnal employment could usually keep juvenile adolescents off thoroughfares during the night hours, including but not limited to the time prior to midnight on weeknights and/or 2 a.m. on weekends.

And the original, using stronger, simpler words:

More night jobs would keep youths off the streets.

In making your word choices, pick the familiar or frequently used word over the unusual or obscure. There are many lists of complex words and suggested substitutes, for example www.plainlanguage.gov/howto/wordsuggestions/simplewords.cfm. See also the lists in Kimble (2006).

Sources
- Kimble, Joseph, *Lifting the Fog of Legalese*, 2006, Carolina Academic Press, Durham, NC, pp. 11, 165-174.
- McGinty, Kathy, *Nine Easy Steps to Longer Sentences*, www.plainlanguage.gov/examples/humor/9easysteps.cfm.

ii. Omit unnecessary words

Wordy, dense construction is one of the biggest problems in government writing. Nothing is more confusing to the user than long, complex sentences containing multiple phrases and clauses. Unnecessary words come in all shapes and sizes, and it's difficult to put them into distinct categories. To address the problem, writers must become more critical of their own writing. They must consider whether they need every word.

Unnecessary words waste your audience's time on the web as well. Remember, great web content is like a conversation. Omit information that the audience doesn't need to know. This can be difficult for a subject matter expert, so it is important to have someone look at the information from the audience's perspective. (See Write web content for more information on writing for the web.)

One place to start working on this problem in your own writing is to watch out for "of," "to," "on," and other ***prepositions***. They often mark phases you can reduce to one or two words.

Don't say	Say
a number of	several, a few, many
a sufficient number of	enough
at this point in time	now
is able to	can
on a monthly basis	monthly

Don't say	Say
on the ground that an amount of X be responsible for in order to	because X must to

Often, you can omit *redundant words*.

Don't say	Say
The X Department and the Y Department worked together on a joint project to improve …	The X and Y Departments worked on a project to improve …

In this statement, you don't need "joint." You don't even need "together." Saying that X *and* Y worked on a project says it all. "Joint" and "together" are both redundant.

Similarly, we often use **excess modifiers** such as *absolutely, actually, completely, really, quite, totally,* and *very*. But if you look closely, you'll find that they often aren't necessary and may even be nonsensical.

Don't say	Say
Their claim was totally unrealistic.	Their claim was absurd.
It is particularly difficult to reconcile the somewhat differing views expressed by the management team.	It is difficult to reconcile the differing views expressed by the management team.
Total disclosure of all facts is very important to make sure we draw up a total and completely accurate picture of the Agency's financial position.	Disclosing all facts is important to creating an accurate picture of the Agency's financial position.

Avoid *doublets and triplets*. English writers love to repeat the same concept by using different words that say the same thing.

Don't say	Say
due and payable	due
cease and desist	stop
knowledge and information	(either one)
begin and commence	start

Other ways to omit unnecessary words include eliminating hidden verbs, using pronouns, and using active voice. See the guidance on those three topics (Avoid hidden verbs, Use pronouns to speak directly to readers, and Use active voice) for more information.

Here's an example that uses several of the techniques discussed above to cut a 54 word sentence down to 22 words, with no loss of meaning.

Don't say	Say
If the State Secretary finds that an individual has received a payment to which the individual was not entitled, whether or not the payment was due to the individual's fault or misrepresentation, the individual shall be liable to repay to State the total sum of the payment to which the individual was not entitled.	If the State Secretary finds that you received a payment that you weren't entitled to, you must pay the entire sum back.

Omitting excess words can cut documents significantly. Be diligent in challenging every word you write, and eventually you will learn to write not only clearly, but concisely.

Sources
- Garner, Bryan A., *Legal Writing in Plain English*, 2001, University of Chicago Press, Chicago, pp. 43, 40, 34.
- Kimble, Joseph, *Lifting the Fog of Legalese,* Carolina Academic Press, 2006, Durham, NC, pp. 93, 170.
- Securities and Exchange Commission, *Plain English Handbook*, 1998, Washington, DC, p. 25.

iii. Dealing with definitions

We have ONE rule for dealing with definitions: ***use them rarely***.

Definitions often cause more problems than they solve. Uniformly, writing experts advise keeping definitions to a minimum (Dickerson 1986, Garner 2001, Kimble 2006). If you can't avoid them, use as few as possible. It's better to take the time to rewrite to avoid needing to define a term. If you must use definitions, follow the guidelines below:

Give common words their common meanings and don't define them.

Never define a word to mean something other than its commonly accepted meaning.

Reed Dickerson, in his landmark book, *Fundamentals of Legal Drafting* (1986), has this advice for legal drafters:

> It is important for the legal draftsman not to define a word in a sense significantly different from the way it is normally understood by the persons to whom it is primarily addressed. This is a fundamental principle of communication, and it is one of the shames of the legal profession that draftsmen so flagrantly violate it. Indeed, the principle is one of the most important in the whole field of legal drafting.

Mr. Dickerson's advice applies to any government communication, not just to legal drafters.

Morris Cohen, in *Reason and Law* (1950), explains, "Whenever we define a word … in a manner that departs from current customary usage, we sooner or later unwittingly fall back on the common use and thus confuse the meanings of our terms."

Furthermore, readers are likely to forget that you'd assigned some common word a new meaning, and when they come upon the word later in your document they assign the common meaning, rather than your specialized one. Here are some unnecessary definitions.

Commonly understood words you probably didn't need to define
Bicycle means every device propelled solely by human power upon which a person or persons may ride on land, having one, two, or more wheels, except a manual wheelchair.
Degrade means to lessen or diminish in quantity, quality, or value.
Age means how old a person is, or the number of elapsed years from the date of a person's birth.

And here are some examples of definitions that conflict with customary usage – you should avoid these at all costs.

Commonly understood words with uncommon meanings	How uncommon meanings might confuse readers
Pages means paper copies of standard office size or the dollar value equivalent in other media	Ten pages into the document, how do you think the average user would respond if asked to define "page"?
Coal deposits mean all Federally owned coal deposits, except those held in trust for a Native American tribe.	So if coal is held in trust for a Native American tribe, it isn't coal?
Dead livestock. The body (cadaver) of livestock which has died otherwise than by slaughter.	So if you slaughter it, it isn't really dead?

When possible, define a word where you use it

Avoid long sections of definitions at the beginning or end of your document. Go back to Rule One. Rewrite to try to eliminate the need for most definitions.

If you must have a definition section, put it at the beginning or the end

Place definitions at the end, in spite of tradition. In placing definitions at the end, you allow your user to go right to the text, rather than having to go through less important material. In definition sections, don't number the definitions, but list them alphabetically. This makes it easier for users to find a definition, and usually makes it easier for you to change your definition section later.

Never include regulatory or other substantive material in definitions

Not only is this common sense — your user doesn't expect substantive material in the definitions section — but for regulations it's a requirement of the Office of the Federal Register.

Consider this "definition" in Title 43 Part 3480 — Coal Exploration and Mining Operations:

> *Maximum economic recovery (MER)* means that, based on standard industry operating practices, all profitable portions of a leased Federal coal deposit must be mined. At the times of MER determinations, consideration will be given to: existing proven technology; commercially available and economically feasible equipment; coal quality, quantity, and marketability; safety, exploration, operating, processing, and transportation costs; and compliance with applicable laws and regulations. The requirement of MER does not restrict the authority of the authorized officer to ensure the conservation of the recoverable coal reserves and other resources and to prevent the wasting of coal.

Hiding in this long passage is the definition, "Maximum economic recovery (MER) means the mining of all profitable portions of a leased Federal coal deposit, based on standard industry operating practices." All the rest of the material belongs in the substantive parts of the regulation.

Don't define words you don't use

Again, this seems obvious. But writers seem to automatically define terms they think they might use, but don't. This can be very confusing for the audience, who expects to read something about the topic but can't find it in the document.

Sources
- Cohen, Morris, *Reason and Law*, 1950, The Free Press, Glencoe, IL, p.77.
- Dickerson, Reed, *Fundamentals of Legal Drafting*, 1986, 2nd edition, Little, Brown and Company, Boston and Toronto, pp. 137, 144.
- Flesch, Rudolf, *How to Write in Plain English, A Book for Lawyers and Consumers*, 1979, Harper and Rowe, New York, pp. 58-69, 79.
- Garner, Bryan A., *A Dictionary of Modern Legal Usage*, 2nd edition, 1995, Oxford University Press, Oxford and New York, p. 257-258.
- Garner, Bryan A., *Legal Writing in Plain English*, 2001, University of Chicago Press, Chicago, pp. 97-99.
- Kimble, Joseph, *Lifting the Fog of Legalese*, Carolina Academic Press, 2006, Durham, NC.
- Office of the Federal Register, Document Drafting Handbook, 1998, § 8.15. www.archives.gov/federal-register/write/handbook/ddh.pdf.

iv. Use the same term consistently for a specific thought or object

You will confuse your audience if you use different terms for the same concept. For example, if you use the term "senior citizens" to refer to a group, continue to use this term throughout your document. Don't substitute another term, such as "the elderly" or "the aged." Using a different term may cause the reader to wonder if you are referring to the same group.

Don't feel that you need to use synonyms to make your writing more interesting. Federal writers are not supposed to be creating great literature. You are communicating requirements, how to get benefits, how to stay safe and healthy, and other information to help people in their lives. While using different words may make writing more interesting, it may decrease clarity.

v. Avoid legal, foreign, and technical jargon

What do we mean by jargon? Jargon is unnecessarily complicated, technical language used to impress, rather than to inform, your audience.

When we say not to use jargon, we're not advocating leaving out necessary technical terms; we are saying to make sure your other language is as clear as possible. For example, there may not be another correct way to refer to a brinulator valve control ring. But that doesn't prevent you from saying "tighten the brinulator valve control ring securely" instead of "Apply sufficient torque to the brinulator valve control ring to ensure that the control ring assembly is securely attached to the terminal such that loosening cannot occur under normal conditions." The first is a necessary use of a technical term. The second is jargon.

Special terms can be useful shorthand within a group and may be the clearest way to communicate inside the group. However, going beyond necessary technical terms to write in jargon can cause misunderstanding or alienation, even if your only readers are specialists. Readers complain about jargon more than any other writing fault, because writers often fail to realize that terms they know well may be difficult or meaningless to their audience. Try to substitute everyday language for jargon as often as possible.

Consider the following pairs. The plainer version conveys technical information just as accurately as and more clearly than the jargon-laden version.

Don't say	Say
riverine avifauna	river birds
involuntarily undomiciled	homeless
The patient is being given positive-pressure ventilatory support.	The patient is on a respirator.
Most refractory coatings to date exhibit a lack of reliability when subject to the impingement of entrained particulate matter in the propellant stream under extended firing durations.	The exhaust gas eventually damages the coating of most existing ceramics.

When you have no way to express an idea except to use technical language, make sure you define your terms. However, it's best to keep definitions to a minimum. Remember to write to communicate, not to impress. If you do that, you should naturally use less jargon. For more on definitions, see Dealing with definitions.

Legal language

Legal language in regulations and other documents is a major source of annoying jargon. Readers can do without archaic jargon such as "hereafter," "heretofore," and "therewith." Professor Joseph Kimble (2006), a noted scholar on legal writing, warns that we should avoid those words and formalisms that give legal writing its musty smell. He includes in his list of examples the following words:

above-mentioned	thereafter
aforementioned	thereof
foregoing	therewith
henceforth	whatsoever
hereafter	whereat
hereby	wherein
herewith	whereof

Another term that is losing its popularity in legal circles is "shall." Obviously, it's especially important in regulations to use words of authority clearly, and many top legal writing experts now recommend avoiding the archaic and ambiguous "shall" in favor of another word, depending on your meaning. Read more about "shall" in Use "must" to convey requirements.

Sources
- Charrow, Veda R., Erhardt, Myra K. and Charrow, Robert P. *Clear & Effective Legal Writing*, 4th edition, 2007, Aspen Publishers, New York, NY, pp. 188-191.
- Garner, Bryan A., *Garner's Modern American Usage*, 2003, Oxford University Press, Oxford and New York, pp. 472-473.
- Kimble, Joseph, *Lifting the Fog of Legalese*, 2006, Carolina Academic Press, Durham, NC, pp.173-174.

vi. Don't use slashes

Apart from fractions, the slash has almost no good uses. "And/or" is a classic example. In most cases, writers mean *either* "or" or "and." But they don't want to take the time to decide which they mean, so they push the job off on the audience. That makes their writing ambiguous. As an author, you should decide what you mean. In the few cases — and there do seem to be very few — where you truly mean both, write out "either X, or Y, or both."

Often when writers use slashes, a hyphen is more appropriate to join equal or like terms, as in "faculty-student ratio."

Sources
- Garner, Bryan A., *Legal Writing in Plain English*, 2001, University of Chicago Press, Chicago, p. 163.
- Kimble, Joseph, *Lifting the Fog of Legalese*, 2006, Carolina Academic Press, Durham, NC, pp. 155-156.

b. Sentences

Choose your words carefully. Start with your main idea – don't start with an exception. Word order does matter, so place your words carefully. Keep it short; it's not a crime to use lots of periods.

1. Write short sentences

Express only one idea in each sentence. Long, complicated sentences often mean that you aren't sure about what you want to say. Shorter sentences are also better for conveying complex information; they break the information up into smaller, easier-to-process units.

Sentences loaded with dependent clauses and exceptions confuse the audience by losing the main point in a forest of words. Resist the temptation to put everything in one sentence; break up your idea into its parts and make each one the subject of its own sentence.

Don't say	Say
Once the candidate's goals are established, one or more potential employers are identified. A preliminary proposal for presentation to the employer is developed. The proposal is presented to an employer who agrees to negotiate an individualized job that meets the employment needs of the applicant and real business needs of the employer.	Once we establish your goals, we identify one or more potential employers. We prepare a preliminary proposal to present to an employer who agrees to negotiate a job that meets both his and your employment needs.

Complexity is the greatest enemy of clear communication. You may need to be especially inventive to translate complicated provisions into more manageable language. In the following example, we have made an "if" clause into a separate sentence. By beginning the first sentence with "suppose" (that is, "if") and the second sentence with "in this case" (that is, "then") we have preserved the relationship between the two.

Don't say	Say
If you take less than your entitled share of production for any month, but you pay royalties on the full volume of your entitled share in accordance with the provisions of this section, you will owe no additional royalty for that lease for prior periods when you later take more than your entitled share to balance your account. This also applies when the other participants pay you money to balance your account.	Suppose that one month you pay royalties on your full share of production but take less than your entitled share. In this case, you may balance your account in one of the following ways without having to pay more royalty. You may either: a. Take more than your entitled share in the future; or b. Accept payment from other participants.

Sources

- Charrow, Veda R., Erhardt, Myra K. and Charrow, Robert P. *Clear & Effective Legal Writing,* 4th edition, 2007, Aspen Publishers, New York, NY, pp. 163-165.
- Garner, Bryan A., *Legal Writing in Plain English*, 2001, University of Chicago Press, Chicago, pp. 19-21.
- Kimble, Joseph, *Guiding Principles for Restyling the Federal Rules of Civil Procedure (Part 1),* Michigan Bar Journal, September 2005, pp. 56-57. www.michbar.org/journal/pdf/pdf4article909.pdf.
- Kimble, Joseph, *Lifting the Fog of Legalese,* 2006, Carolina Academic Press, Durham, NC, p. 96.
- Murawski, Thomas A., *Writing Readable Regulations*, 1999, Carolina Academic Press Durham, NC, p. 77.
- Office of the Federal Register, *Document Drafting Handbook*, 1998, MMR-5. www.archives.gov/federal-register/write/handbook/ddh.pdf.
- Redish, Janice C., *How to Write Regulations and Other Legal Documents in Clear English*, 1991, American Institutes for Research, Washington, DC, pp. 29-32
- Securities and Exchange Commission, *Plain English Handbook*, 1998, Washington, DC, p. 28.

2. Keep subject, verb, and object close together

The natural word order of an English sentence is subject-verb-object. This is how you first learned to write sentences, and it's still the best. When you put modifiers, phrases, or clauses between two or all three of these essential parts, you make it harder for the user to understand you.

Consider this long, convoluted sentence:

> If any member of the board retires, the company, at the discretion of the board, and after notice from the chairman of the board to all the members of the board at least 30 days before executing this option, may buy, and the retiring member must sell, the member's interest in the company.

In essence, the sentence says:

> The company may buy a retiring member's interest.

All the rest of the material modifies the basic idea, and should be moved to another sentence or at least to the end of the sentence.

Many sentences in regulations include "if-then" provisions. Often, "if" defines who is covered by a provision. Start your sentence with the "if" provision, and then list the "then" provisions. If the provision is complex, and especially if there are several different "if" provisions, use a different sentence for every "if," or consider using an if-then table.

Consider this complex regulatory provision:

> We must receive your completed application form on or before the 15th day of the second month following the month you are reporting if you do not submit your application electronically or the 25th day of the second month following the month you are reporting if you submit your application electronically.

While still complex, the table is a significant improvement:

We must receive your completed application by the following dates:

If you submit your form ...	We must receive it by ...
Electronically	the 25th of the second month following the month you are reporting
Other than electronically	the 15th of the second month following the month you are reporting

For more information on tables, see Use tables to make complex material easier to understand.

Sources

- Garner, Bryan A., *Legal Writing in Plain English*, 2001, University of Chicago Press, Chicago, pp. 23-24, 102.
- Murawski, Thomas A., *Writing Readable Regulations*, 1999, Carolina Academic Press Durham, NC, pp. 77-78.
- Office of the Federal Register, *Document Drafting Handbook*, 1998, MMR-6. www.archives.gov/federal-register/write/handbook/ddh.pdf
- Securities and Exchange Commission, *Plain English Handbook*, 1998, Washington, DC, p. 32.

3. Avoid double negatives and exceptions to exceptions

We're accustomed to thinking and speaking positively. When we write in the negative, we place another stumbling block in audience's way and make it more difficult for them to understand us. When you're going to meet a friend at the airport, do you say, "If you fail to arrive by 5:00, I cannot pick you up," or do you say, "You have to arrive by 5:00 if you want me to pick you up"?

When you write a sentence containing two negatives, they cancel each other out. Your sentence sounds negative, but is actually positive. As Rudolph Flesch (1979) says, these sentences require "a mental switch from no to yes."

Don't say	Say
No approval of any noise compatibility program, or any portion of a program, may be implied **in the absence of** the agency's express approval.	You must get the agency's express approval for any noise compatibility program or any portion of a program.

Here are some expressions that signal double negatives.

Change the double negative	To a positive
no fewer than …	at least
has not yet attained	is under
may not … until	may only … when
is not … unless	is … only if

Many ordinary words have a negative meaning, such as *unless, fail to, notwithstanding, except, other than, unlawful (un-* words), *disallowed (dis-* words), *terminate, void, insufficient,* and so on. Watch out for them when they appear after ***not***. Find a positive word to express your meaning.

Don't say	Say
An application for a grant does not become void unless the applicant's failure to provide requested information is unreasonable under the circumstances.	An application for a grant remains active if the applicant provides the information we request within a reasonable time.

Exceptions to exceptions

An exception that contains an exception is just another form of a double negative. That makes it even harder for the user to puzzle out. Rewrite the sentence to emphasize the positive.

Don't say	Say
Applicants may be granted a permit to prospect for geothermal resources on any federal lands except lands in the National Park System, unless the applicant holds valid existing rights to the geothermal resources on the National Park System lands listed in the application.	You may be granted a permit to prospect for geothermal resources on any federal lands. This includes lands in the National Park System only if you hold valid existing rights to the park lands listed in your application.

Sources
- Charrow, Veda R., Erhardt, Myra K. and Charrow, Robert P. *Clear & Effective Legal Writing,* 4th edition, 2007, Aspen Publishers, New York, NY, pp. 178-180.
- Flesch, Rudolf, How to Write in Plain English, A Book for Lawyers and Consumers, 1979, Harper and Rowe, New York, p. 95.
- Garner, Bryan A., *Guidelines for Drafting and Editing Court Rules,* 1996, Administrative Office of the US Courts, Washington, DC, pp. 30-31.
- Wydick, Richard, *Plain English for Lawyers,* 5th edition, 2005, Carolina Academic Press, Durham, NC, pp. 75-76.

4. Place the main idea before exceptions and conditions

When you start a sentence with an introductory phrase or clause beginning with "except," you almost certainly force the reader to re-read your sentence. You are stating an exception to a rule before you have stated the underlying rule. The audience must absorb the exception, then the rule, and then usually has to go back to grasp the relationship between the two. Material is much easier to follow if you start with the main idea and then cover exceptions and conditions.

Don't say	Say
Except as described in paragraph (b), the Division Manager will not begin the statutory 180-day review period for the program until after the preliminary review determines that your submission is administratively complete.	The Division Manager will not begin the statutory 180-day review period for the program until the preliminary review determines that your submission is administratively complete. However, see paragraph (b) for an exception.

In the first version, the audience has to decide whether to jump immediately down to paragraph (b) or continue reading to the end of the sentence. This means the audience is focusing on reading strategy, not on your content.

There is no absolute rule about where to put exceptions and conditions. Put them where they can be absorbed most easily by readers. In general, the main point of the sentence should be as close to the beginning as possible.

Usually use the word *if* for conditions. Use *when* (not *where*), if you need *if* to introduce another clause or if the condition occurs regularly.

If an exception or condition is just *a few words*, and seeing it first will avoid misleading users, put it at the beginning instead of the end.

Don't say	Say
With your grant application you must submit a resume containing your	*Unless you have already submitted an up-to-date resume*, you must submit a

Don't say	Say
undergraduate, graduate, and any other professional education, your work experience in the field of health care, and the name, and phone number of current and previous employers in the health care field, ***unless you have already submitted this information***.	resume containing your undergraduate, graduate, and any other professional education, your work experience in the field of health care, and the name, address and phone number of current and previous employers in the health care field.

If an exception or condition is *long* and the main clause is *short*, put the main clause first and then state the exception or condition.

Don't say	Say
Except when you submitted an identical application for an education grant in the previous year and you received full or partial grant for that year's program, we will schedule a hearing on your application.	We will schedule a hearing on your application, ***except when you submitted an identical application for an education grant in the previous year and you received full or partial grant for that year's program***.

If a condition and the main clause are ***both long***, *foreshadow* the condition and put it at the end of the sentence. If there are several conditions, lead with "*if*" or a phrase such as "*in the following circumstances*."

Don't say	Say
If you, or an interested party, requests that the hearing be held at the educational institution where you plan to instruct program participants, and the hearing room is both handicapped-accessible and large enough for at least 100 people, we may, at our discretion, hold the hearing at that location, after adequate public notice.	We may hold a hearing at the educational institution where you plan to instruct program participants *if*: a. You, or an interested party, request the location; b. The hearing room is large enough for at least 100 people and handicapped-accessible; and c. We can give adequate public notice.

Use a list (like the example above) if your sentence contains multiple conditions or exceptions. Here's how the first example, above, could be rewritten.

Don't say	Say
With your grant application you must submit a resume containing your undergraduate, graduate, and any other professional education, your work experience in the field of health care, and the name, and phone number of current and previous employers in the health care field, ***unless you have already submitted this information.***	***Unless you have already submitted an up-to-date resume,*** you must submit a resume containing: • Your undergraduate, graduate, and any other professional education; • Your work experience in the field of health care; and • The name, address and phone number of current and previous employers in the health care field.

Use numbers or letters to designate items in a list if future reference or sequence is important (for example, in a regulation). Otherwise, use bullets.

Make implied conditions explicit by using **if**.

Don't say	Say
A party must make advance arrangements with the hearing officer for the transportation and receipt of ***exhibits of unusual bulk.***	***If your exhibits are unusually bulky,*** you must make advance arrangements for transporting them with the hearing.

Avoid using an exception, if you can, by stating a rule or category directly rather than describing that rule or category by stating its exceptions.

Don't say	Say
All persons except those 18 years or older must…	Each person under 18 years of age must…

But use an exception if it avoids a long and cumbersome list or elaborate description.

Don't say	Say
Alabama, Alaska,… and Wyoming (a list of 47 states) must	Each state except Texas, New Mexico, and Arizona must…

Sources

- Charrow, Veda R., Erhardt, Myra K. and Charrow, Robert P. *Clear & Effective Legal Writing,* 4th edition, 2007, Aspen Publishers, New York, NY, pp. 166-167.
- Garner, Bryan A., *Guidelines for Drafting and Editing Court Rules,* 1996, Administrative Office of the US Courts, Washington, DC, pp. 5-9.
- Office of the Federal Register, *Drafting Legal Documents,* 1998, § 7. www.archives.gov/federal-register/write/legal-docs/
- Wydick, Richard, *Plain English for Lawyers,* 5th edition, 2005, Carolina Academic Press, Durham, NC, pp. 46-47.

5. Place words carefully

Sloppy word placement can cause ambiguity. To reduce ambiguity:

- Keep subjects and objects close to their verbs.

- Put conditionals such as "only" or "always" and other modifiers next to the words they modify. Write "you are required to provide only the following," not "you are only required to provide the following."

- Put long conditions after the main clause. Write "complete form 9-123 if you own more than 50 acres and cultivate grapes," not "if you own more than 50 acres and cultivate grapes, complete form 9-123."

In the left column below, it's difficult to figure out which words relate to the forest products, which to the tribe, and which to the payments. The right column eliminates this problem by dividing the material into shorter sentences and pulling together the words about each provision.

Confusing word placement	Clearer construction
Upon the request of an Indian tribe, the Secretary may provide that the purchaser of the forest products of such tribe, which are harvested under a timber sale contract,	If a tribe (you) asks us, we will require purchasers of your forest products to deposit their payment into an account

Confusing word placement	Clearer construction
permit, or other harvest sale document, make advance deposits, or direct payments of the gross proceeds of such forest products, less any amounts segregated as forest management deductions pursuant to section 163.25, into accounts designated by such Indian tribe.	that you designate. a. You can instruct us to deposit advance payments as well as direct payments into the account. b. We will withhold from the deposit any forest management deductions under section 163.25.

You will eliminate many potential sources of ambiguity by writing shorter sentences. The less complex the sentence, the clearer the meaning and less chance that ambiguity will creep in. Still, you must watch how you place words even in short sentences. In the example below, the audience may have to read the original statement several times to realize that we don't mean, "If you really want to have a disability …"

Ambiguous construction	Clearer construction
If you are determined to have a disability, we will pay you the following:	If we determine that you have a disability, we will pay you the following:

Sources

- Garner, Bryan A., *Garner's Modern American Usage,* 2003, Oxford University Press, Oxford and New York, pp. 566-567.

c. Paragraphs

Write short paragraphs and include only one topic in each paragraph.

1. Have a topic sentence

If you tell your readers what they're going to read about, they're less likely to have to read your paragraph again. Headings help, but they're not enough. Establish a context for your audience before you provide them with the details. If you flood readers with details first, they become impatient and may resist hearing your message. A good topic sentence draws the audience into your paragraph.

We often write the way we think, putting our premises first and then our conclusion. It may be the natural way to develop our thoughts, but we wind up with the topic sentence at the end of the paragraph. Move it up front and let users know where you're going. Don't make readers hold a lot of information in their heads before they get to your point.

Also, busy readers want to *skim* your document, stopping only for what they want or need to know. You can help them by giving each paragraph a good introduction. Readers should be able to get good general understanding of your document by skimming your topic sentences.

A side benefit of good topic sentences (and good headings) is that they help you see if your document is well-organized. If it isn't, topic sentences make it easier for you to rearrange your material.

Sources
- Garner, Bryan A., *Legal Writing in Plain English*, 2001, University of Chicago Press, Chicago, pp. 65-66.

2. Use transition words

A topic sentence may provide a transition from one paragraph to another. But a transition word or phrase (usually in the topic sentence) clearly tells the audience whether the paragraph expands on the paragraph before, contrasts with it, or takes a completely different direction.

Bryan Garner (2001) divides transition words into three types:

Pointing words: words like *this, that, these, those,* and *the.*

Pointing words – especially *this* and *that* — refer directly to something already mentioned. They point to an antecedent. If your preceding paragraph describes the process of strip mining, and your next paragraph begins with "this process causes…," the word *this* makes a clear connection between paragraphs.

*Echo links***:** words or phrases echo a previously mentioned idea.

Echo links often work together with pointing words. In the example above, you've just written a paragraph about how strip mining removes the top surface of the land to get at the coal under it. If you then begin the next paragraph with "this scarring of the earth," the words "scarring of the earth" are an echo of the mining process described in the previous paragraph.

Explicit connectives: words whose chief purpose is to supply transitions (such as *further, also, therefore*).

Explicit connectives between sentences and paragraphs can be overdone, but more often we simply overlook using them. Being too familiar with our own material, we think they aren't needed. Readers, on the other hand, find them helpful in following our train of thought. Here are some examples from Bryan Garner.

- ***When adding a point***: also, and, in addition, besides, what is more, similarly, further

- ***When giving an example***: for instance, for example, for one thing, for another thing

- ***When restating***: in other words, that is, in short, put differently, again

- ***When introducing a result***: so, as a result, thus, therefore, accordingly, then

- ***When contrasting***: but, however, on the other hand, still, nevertheless, conversely

- ***When summing up***: to summarize, to sum up, to conclude, in conclusion, in short

- ***When sequencing ideas***: First,…Second,…Third,…Finally,…

Sources
- Garner, Bryan A., *Legal Writing in Plain English*, 2001, University of Chicago Press, Chicago, pp. 67-71.

3. Write short paragraphs

Long paragraphs discourage your audience from even trying to understand your material. Short paragraphs are easier to read and understand. Writing experts recommend paragraphs of no more than 150 words in three to eight sentences. Paragraphs should never be longer than 250 words. Vary the lengths of your paragraphs to make them more interesting. As with sentence length, if all paragraphs are the same size your writing will be choppy.

There is nothing wrong with an occasional one-sentence paragraph.

Using short paragraphs is an ideal way to open up your document and create more white space. In turn, this makes your writing more inviting and easier to read. It also gives you the opportunity to add more headings.

Long, dense paragraph	Material divided into four paragraphs
Flu Medication A specific vaccine for humans that is effective in preventing avian influenza is not yet readily available. Based upon limited data, the CDC has suggested that the anti-viral medication Oseltamivir (brand name-Tamiflu) may be effective in treating avian influenza. Using this input, the Department of State has decided to pre-position the drug Tamiflu at its Embassies and Consulates worldwide, for eligible U.S. Government employees and their families serving abroad who become ill with avian influenza. We emphasize that this medication cannot be made available to private U.S. citizens abroad. Because of this, and because Tamiflu may not be readily available overseas, the State Department encourages American citizens traveling or living abroad to consult with their private physician about whether to obtain Tamiflu prior to travel, for use in the event treatment becomes necessary, or whether Tamiflu is readily available in the country where they reside. Americans should also be aware of the potential health risk posed by counterfeit drugs, including those represented as Tamiflu, by internet scam artists or in countries with lax regulations governing the production	**Flu Medication for Government Employees** A specific vaccine for humans effective in preventing avian influenza is not yet readily available. Based on limited data, the CDC suggested that the anti-viral medication Oseltamivir (brand name-Tamiflu) may be effective in treating avian influenza. Using this input, the Department of State decided to pre-position the drug Tamiflu at its Embassies and Consulates worldwide, for eligible U.S. Government employees and their families serving abroad who become ill with avian influenza. **Flu Medication for Private Citizens** We emphasize that we can't make this medication available to private U.S. citizens abroad. Because of this, and because Tamiflu may not be readily available overseas, the State Department encourages American citizens traveling or living abroad to consult with their private physician about whether to get Tamiflu before they travel, whether to use if treatment becomes necessary, or if Tamiflu is readily available in the country where they live. **Counterfeit Drug Warning** Americans should also be aware of the

Long, dense paragraph	Material divided into four paragraphs
and distribution of pharmaceuticals. In addition, the Department of State has asked its embassies and consulates to consider preparedness measures that take into consideration the fact that travel into or out of a country may not be possible, safe or medically advisable. Guidance on how private citizens can prepare for a "stay in place" response, including stockpiling food, water, and medical supplies, is available on the CDC and pandemicflu.gov websites.	potential health risk posed by counterfeit drugs, including those represented as Tamiflu, by internet scam artists or in countries with lax regulations governing the production and distribution of pharmaceuticals. **Additional Precautions** In addition, the Department of State has asked its embassies and consulates to consider preparedness measures that consider that travel into or out of a country may not be possible, safe or medically advisable. Guidance on how private citizens can prepare for a "stay in place" response, including stockpiling food, water, and medical supplies, is available on the CDC and pandemicflu.gov websites.

In addition to breaking material into more, shorter, paragraphs, consider using a heading for each paragraph, as we did in this example.

See also Cover only one topic in each paragraph.

Sources
- Garner, Bryan A., *Legal Writing in Plain English*, 2001, University of Chicago Press, Chicago, pp. 72-73.
- Murawski, Thomas A., *Writing Readable Regulations*, 1999, Carolina Academic Press Durham, NC, pp. 24-25.

4. Cover only one topic in each paragraph

Limit each paragraph or section to one topic to make it easier for your audience to understand your information. Each paragraph should start with a topic sentence that captures the essence of everything in the paragraph.

Don't say	Say
a. Notice of a bid advertisement shall be published in at least one local newspaper and in one trade publication at least 30 days in advance of sale. If applicable, the notice must identify the reservation within which the tracts to be leased are found. Specific descriptions of the tracts shall be available at the office of the superintendent. The complete text of the advertisement shall be mailed to each person listed on the appropriate agency mailing list.	a. Thirty days before the sale, we will publish a notice advertising bids. The notice will be in at least one local newspaper and in one trade publication. It will identify any reservation where the tracts to be leased are located. b. We will share information about this process in two other ways. We will mail the advertisement to each person on the appropriate agency mailing list. We will also provide specific descriptions of the tracts at the superintendent's office.

Putting each topic in a separate paragraph makes your information easier to digest.

d. Other aids to clarity

Examples help your readers understand your points. Break up lots of text with lists and tables. Including an illustration can be more helpful than describing it.

1. Use examples

Examples help you clarify complex concepts, even in regulations. They are an ideal way to help your readers. In spoken English, when you ask for clarification of something, people often respond by giving you an example. Good examples can substitute for long explanations. The more complex the concept you are writing about, the more you should consider using an example. By giving your audience an example that's relevant to their situation, you help them relate to your document.

Avoid using the Latin abbreviations for "for example" (e.g.) and "that is" (i.e.). Few people know what they mean, and they often confuse the two. Write out the lead-in to your example: "for example" or "such as."

The Internal Revenue Service makes extensive use of examples in its regulations throughout 26 CFR Part 1, the regulations on income taxes. The Environmental Protection Agency also uses examples in its regulations. Here's one from 40 CFR Part 50, Appendix H – Interpretation of the 1-Hour Primary and Secondary National Ambient Air Quality Standards for Ozone.

EPA example
Suppose a monitoring station records a valid daily maximum hourly average ozone value for every day of the year during the past 3 years. At the end of each year, the number of days with maximum hourly concentrations above 0.12 ppm is determined and this number is averaged with the results of previous years. As long as this average remains "less than or equal to 1," the area is in compliance.

Sources
- Murawski, Thomas A., *Writing Readable Regulations*, 1999, Carolina Academic Press Durham, NC, pp. 45-46.

2. Use lists

Vertical lists highlight a series of requirements or other information in a visually clear way. Use vertical lists to help your user focus on important material. Vertical lists:

- Highlight levels of importance

- Help the user understand the order in which things happen

- Make it easy for the user to identify all necessary steps in a process

- Add blank space for easy reading

- Are an ideal way to present items, conditions, and exceptions

Don't say	Say
Each completed well drilling application must contain a detailed statement including the following information: the depth of the well, the casing and cementing program, the circulation media (mud, air, foam, etc.), the expected depth and thickness of fresh water zones, and well site layout and design.	With your application for a drilling permit, provide the following information: • Depth of the well; • Casing and cementing program; • Circulation media (mud, air, form, etc); • Expected depth and thickness of fresh water zones; and • Well site layout and design.

Vertical lists are also helpful in clarifying the chronological order of steps in a process. With these lists, consider numbering the items to suggest the order of steps.

Vertical list suggests the correct order of events
When a foreign student presents a completed Form I-20: 1. Enter the student's admission number from Form 94; 2. Endorse all copies of the form; 3. Return a copy to the student; and 4. Send a copy to the Immigration and Naturalization Service.

However, you can over-use vertical lists. Remember to use them to highlight important information, not to over-emphasize trivial matters. If you use bullets, use solid round or square ones. Bullets are not the place to be overly creative. Large creative bullets with strange shapes tend to distract the reader and may not display properly on some computer systems.

Your lists will be easier to read if you:

- Always use a lead-in sentence to explain your lists;
- Indent your lead-in sentence from the left margin; and
- Use left justification only – never center justification.

Don't say	Say
Classroom supplies: • A tablet • A pen or pencil • The paperwork you sent us when you first applied for class	Classroom Supplies When you come to class, you should bring the following — • A tablet • A pen or pencil • The paperwork you sent us when you first applied for class.

In the example above, the lack of a lead-in sentence on the left makes it unclear who is to bring the supplies. The lead-in sentence on the right clarifies who is responsible for bringing supplies. Indenting the list under the lead in sentence makes it easier to see how the information is chunked. Use parallel construction and make sure each of the bullets in a list can make a complete sentence if combined with the lead-in sentence.

The following example is a list that is not parallel:

You must submit:

• Your application,
• Recommendation letter, and
• Mail it express mail.

The bullet "Mail it express mail" does not work with the rest of the list. The other items are nouns, but this is a verb. It isn't something to submit. It's a separate part of the instructions.

Sources

• Charrow, Veda R., Erhardt, Myra K. and Charrow, Robert P. *Clear & Effective Legal Writing*, 4th edition, 2007, Aspen Publishers, New York, NY, pp. 181-182.
• Garner, Bryan A., *Legal Writing in Plain English*, 2001, University of Chicago Press, Chicago, pp. 100, 125.
• Murawski, Thomas A., *Writing Readable Regulations*, 1999, Carolina Academic Press Durham, NC, pp. 25, 81-84.
• Securities and Exchange Commission, *Plain English Handbook*, 1998, Washington, DC, p. 34.

3. Use tables to make complex material easier to understand

Tables help your audience see relationships that are often times hidden in dense text. And for most readers, it's not necessary to understand all possibilities and conditions, only those that apply to the reader's situation.

Probably the most useful type of table is the "if-then" table. An "if-then" table organizes the material by a situation (if something is the case) and the consequence (then something else happens). The rewritten regulation in the "if-then" table below is far clearer than the dense text it replaces. It also makes the document appear less dense and easier on the eye.

Dense text from 25 CFR 163.25

§ 163.25 Forest management deductions.

a. Pursuant to the provisions of 25 U.S.C. 413 and 25 U.S.C. 3105, a forest management deduction shall be withheld from the gross proceeds of sales of Indian forest land as described in this section.

b. Gross proceeds shall mean the value in money or money's worth of consideration furnished by the purchaser of forest products purchased under a contract, permit, or other document for the sale of forest products.

c. Forest management deductions shall not be withheld where the total consideration furnished under a document for the sale of forest products is less than $5,001.

d. Except as provided in § 163.25(e) of this part, the amount of the forest deduction shall not exceed the lesser amount of ten percent (10%) of the gross proceeds or, the actual percentage in effect on November 28, 1990.

e. The Secretary may increase the forest management deduction percentage for Indian forest land upon receipt of a written request from a tribe supported by a written resolution executed by the authorized tribal representatives. At the request of the authorized tribal representatives and at the discretion of the Secretary the forest management deduction percentage may be decreased to not less than one percent (1%) or the requirement for collection may be waived.

If-then table

§ 163.25 Will BIA withhold any forest management deductions?

We will withhold a forest management deduction if the contract for the sale of forest products has a value of over $5,000. The deduction will be a percentage of the price we get from the buyer. The following table shows how we determine the amount of the deduction.

If ...	and ...	then the percentage of the deduction is ...
a tribe requests an increase in the deduction through a tribal resolution	they send us a written request	the percentage requested by the tribe.
an authorized tribal representative requests a decrease in the deduction	we approve the decrease	the percentage requested, with a one percent minimum.
an authorized tribal representative requests a waiver of the deduction	we approve the waiver	waived.
none of the above conditions applies		the percentage in effect on November 28, 1990, or 10 percent, whichever is less.

You can use variations on the if-then table to clarify other types of complicated provisions. Which of the following would you rather read?

§ 163.17 Deposit with bid.

(a) A deposit shall be made with each proposal for the purchase of Indian forest products. Such deposits shall be at least:

(1) Ten (10) percent if the appraised stumpage value is less than $100,000 in any event not less than $1,000 or full value whichever is less.
(2) Five (5) percent if the appraised stumpage value is $100,000 to $250,000 but in any event not less than $10,000; and
(3) Three (3) percent if the appraised stumpage value exceeds $250,000 but it any event not less than $12,500.

§ 163.17 Must I make a deposit with my bid?

You must include a deposit with your bid to buy Indian forest products, but the amount of the deposit varies.

If the appraised stumpage value is ...	you must deposit ...	and the minimum amount of the deposit is ...
less than $100,000	ten percent of the stumpage value	$1,000
between $100,000 and $250,000	five percent of the stumpage value	$10,000
over $250,000	three percent of the stumpage value	$12,500

If-then tables are powerful tools for simplifying complicated material. And tables generally use many fewer words that a straight textual explanation would use.

Sources

- Kimble, Joseph, *Lifting the Fog of Legalese*, 2006, Carolina Academic Press, Durham, NC, p. 70(B).
- Murawski, Thomas A., *Writing Readable Regulations*, 1999, Carolina Academic Press Durham, NC, pp. 39-44.
- Office of the Federal Register, *Document Drafting Handbook*, 1998, MMR 4. www.archives.gov/federal-register/write/handbook/.
- Securities and Exchange Commission, *Plain English Handbook*, 1998, Washington, DC, pp. 49-52.

4. Consider using illustrations

While government pamphlets and similar items intended for the public usually include many illustrations, illustrations rarely appear in letters or regulations. However, even in these documents, you can use illustrations to good effect. Consider these examples from regulations.

Federal Aviation Regulations in 14 CFR part 95 contain illustrations of mountainous areas which are subject to special flight restrictions, such as this illustration of mountainous areas of Alaska:

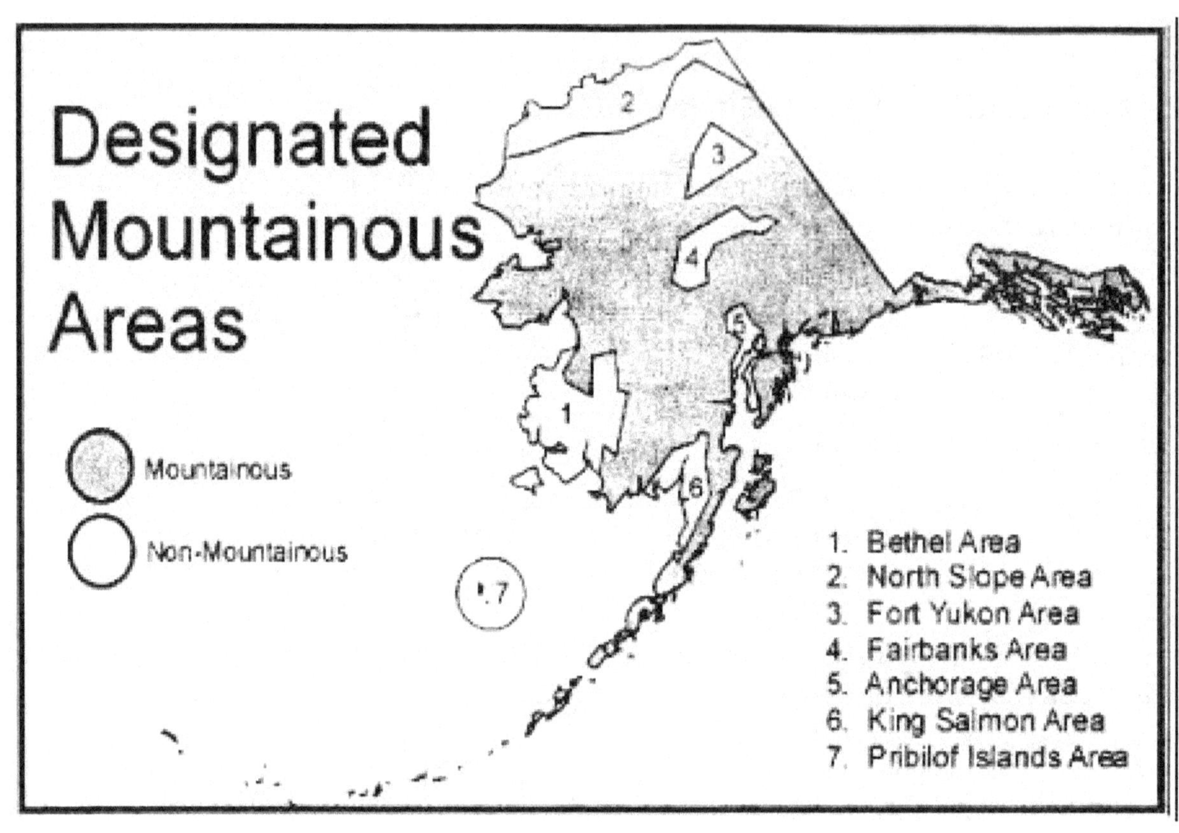

National Park Service regulations at 36 CFR part 7.96 includes pictures of areas in Washington, DC, where activities are controlled, such as these drawings of the White House and Lincoln Memorial:

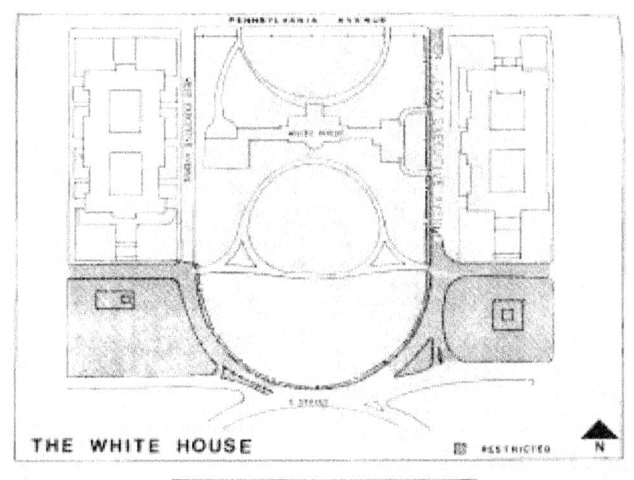

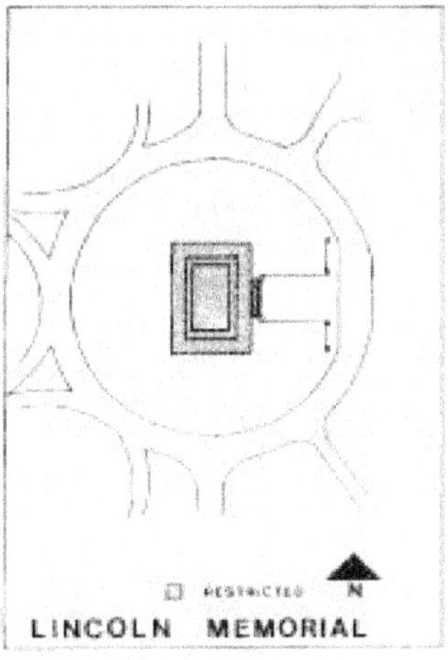

14 CFR 1221.102 establishes the NASA Seal.

The NASA Seal

TECHNICAL DESCRIPTION:

The official seal of the National Aeronautics and Space Administration is a disc of blue sky strewn with white stars. To the left, there is a large yellow sphere bearing a red flight vector symbol. The wings of the vector symbol envelope and cast a brown shadow upon it. A white horizontal orbit also encircles the sphere. To the right, there is a small light blue sphere. A white band which circumscribes the disc is edged in gold and is inscribed with "National Aeronautics and Space Administration U.S.A." in red letters.

Appendix B to 40 CFR Part 50 illustrates the measurement principle and calibration procedure for measuring carbon monoxide in the atmosphere.

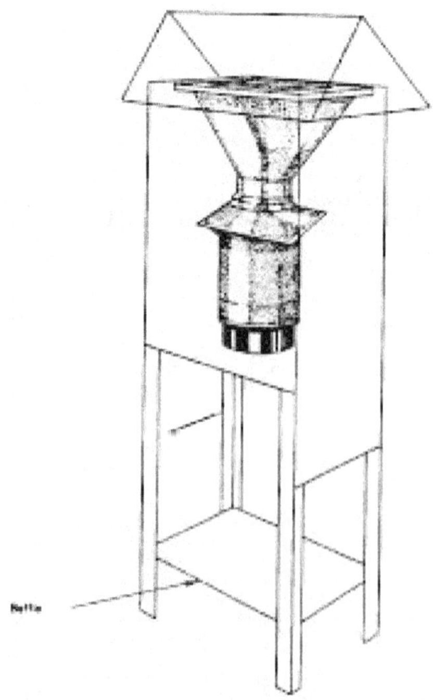

Figure 1. High-volume sampler in shelter.

50 CFR section 216.95 illustrates the official mark for "Dolphin-safe" tuna products.

Figure 1.

5. Use emphasis to highlight important concepts

Use **bold and italics** to make important concepts stand out. While it is difficult to use these techniques in regulations, emphasis helps bring out important points in other documents. Limit emphasis to important information, otherwise you'll dilute its impact.

PUTTING EVERYTHING IN CAPITAL LETTERS IS NOT A GOOD EMPHASIS TECHNIQUE. ALTHOUGH IT MAY DRAW THE USER'S ATTENTION TO THE SECTION, IT MAKES IT HARDER TO READ. AND IN AN ELECTRONIC ENVIRONMENT IT'S CONSIDERED SHOUTING. <u>Similarly, underlining will draw the user's attention to the section, but it makes it hard to read</u>. Besides, in an electronic environment, people expect underlined text to be a link. ***It's better to use bold and italics for important issues.***

6. Minimize cross-references

Nothing is more annoying than coming upon cross-references in reading material. Cross-references frustrate any attempt to write clearly and simply. Most users consider them a bother, and just skip over them. This can be a problem when the document is a regulation. Numerous cross-references can confuse users and make them less attentive to your message. They may also overtax your users' short-term memory. Imagine the work it would take a user to puzzle out just this one short section from our tax regulations (26 CFR 1.1(h)-1).

<table>
<tr><td align="center">Regulation with many confusing cross-references</td></tr>
<tr><td>"Section 1250 capital gain — (i) Definition. For purposes of this section, section 1250 capital gain means the capital gain (not otherwise treated as ordinary income) that would be treated as ordinary income if section 1250(b)(1) included all depreciation and the applicable percentage under section 1250(a) were 100 percent."</td></tr>
</table>

On the other hand, repeating bulky material over and over can be equally annoying to users. So there is a place for cross-references, but the challenge is to not overdo them.

How to minimize cross-references

There are several ways to deal with cross-references. The best is to organize your material so you can **eliminate the need for cross-references**. Often, you are forced to resort to a cross-reference because the material isn't organized the way it should be, so material that belongs together is instead found in distant sections. However, given the complexity of some documents, it won't be possible to eliminate them all. If a cross-reference refers to **brief material**, just repeat that material and get rid of the cross-reference. Sometimes, careful thought may reveal that you've included an **unnecessary cross-reference**.

If the cross-reference is to **lengthy material** that, if included, would make the wording long and complicated, you may have to refer users to another section. Typically, this would include long descriptive material, such as a long list of items or a list of requirements that you want to apply to a new situation.

Be sure that the reference you insert clearly describes the referenced material. That way, users can decide if they need to read it to know how the rule affects them. Sometimes just including the title of the referenced section is enough.

Let's look at an example from the National Park Service.

A requirement with several cross references

Section 45. May I camp in a national park?

If you hold one of the vehicle entry passes listed in Section 18 for entry into a national park, you may camp in that park. But you may not sleep in a tent if the park has declared one of the animal danger levels described in paragraphs (c) through (h) of Section 51, and the campsite is not covered by an animal emergency plan as described in Section 52.

In this excerpt, the first cross-reference is to brief material, so you can just repeat it here. The second cross-reference is to a long list of information; it's probably clearest to keep the cross-reference. The third cross-reference probably isn't necessary — the camper needs to know whether there is an animal emergency plan, but not the details of the plan contained in Section 52. Following these principles, the final text could read:

Two of three cross-references eliminated

Section 45. May I camp in a national park?

If you hold a daily, weekly, or annual vehicle entry pass for a national park, you may camp in that park. But you may not sleep in a tent if the park has declared one of the animal danger levels described in paragraphs (c) through (h) of Section 51, and the campsite is not covered by an animal emergency plan.

Another treatment

If you believe you must include cross-references, consider putting them at the end of the text, like a reference, rather than in the middle. This is less disruptive to the user, and less annoying. It gives users a chance to absorb your main message before your references elaborate on it. As an example, if you need to keep the second and third references in the national park example above, you might write it this way:

Cross-references at end of passage

Section 45. May I camp in a national park?

If you hold a daily, weekly, or annual vehicle entry pass for a national park, you may camp in that park. But you may not sleep in a tent if the park has declared an animal danger level and the campsite is not covered by an animal emergency plan. (See paragraphs (c) through (h) of Section 51 for animal danger levels.) (See Section 52 for animal emergency plans.)

Referring to another agency's regulations

If you want to require users to comply with certain requirements of another federal agency, which they would not otherwise have to do, you have to meet the requirements of the Office of the Federal Register (OFR). A federal agency may cross-reference the regulations of another federal agency only if the OFR finds that the reference meets one of the conditions specified in 1 CFR 21.21. You can find a discussion of these conditions in the OFR's *Drafting Legal Documents* under Cross References.

Referring to other material in regulations

A cross-reference to material that does not appear in the *Federal Register* or the Code of Federal Regulations is called an "incorporation by reference" by the Office of the Federal Register. The OFR has very specific rules that agencies must follow to do incorporation by reference. You will find them in 1 CFR part 51 and Chapter 6 of the OFR's *Document Drafting Handbook.*

Avoid these situations

Multiple cross-references in one section. Multiple cross-references make your user's head spin, and you will fail to deliver any useful information. Reorganize your material to eliminate the cross-references, or at least to keep them to no more than one in each section.

Unnecessary cross references put in to ensure that your users don't miss something that applies to them. You won't know where to stop cross-referencing. You should presume that users will familiarize themselves with your document to see what applies to them. Make sure your table of contents and headings are informative enough that users can find everything they need.

Cross-referencing definitions. Adding a cross-reference to a definition for the convenience of the audience may create a problem if you don't continue to repeat it every time you use the word.

If you say	Then you can't later just say
a corporation as defined in Section 1 (when Section 1 clearly applies to your regulation and defines a corporation as having, for example, at least 50 employees)	a corporation (some users may think the 50-employee limit doesn't apply here.)

The "boomerang." Rudolf Flesch (1979) named this particularly insidious cross-reference. It's a reference that refers to the section it's found in. It sends users on a futile hunt for another section of the same number, until they finally realize you are referring to the same section they were reading in the first place. If you mean "listed in paragraph (h) of this section" say it that way. The Office of the Federal Register's *Document Drafting Handbook* tells you the proper way to refer to something in the same section of a regulation.

The "all-inclusive" cross-reference. It's no help to your audience to say something like "As a permittee, you must comply with sections 542.6 and 543.10, and all other applicable laws and regulations." What exactly does the term "all other applicable laws and regulations" cover? Do you expect your reader to become a legal scholar and go out and research the answer to that question? This form of cross-reference reflects a lazy writer. And it's not likely to achieve much.

The never-ending story cross reference. This is the cross-reference that refers the reader to another section containing another cross-reference, which takes the reader to yet another section containing another cross-reference, and so on forever and ever. If you can't follow the web of references, why do you think your audience will?

Final thoughts

Whether you use a cross-reference or repeat the material in the new location, you must remember to update the information if something in the cross-referenced material changes.

There is no hard and fast rule about when it's reasonable to use a cross-reference. It depends on the purpose of the cross reference and the bulk of the material referenced. The bottom line is that you should minimize them to the extent possible.

Sources
- Flesch, Rudolf, How to Write in Plain English, A Book for Lawyers and Consumers, 1979, Harper and Rowe, New York, pp. 82-93.
- Office of the Federal Register, Document Drafting Handbook, 1998, 1-15. www.archives.gov/federal-register/write/handbook/ddh.pdf.

7. Design your document for easy reading

We want our documents to help the audience get information, comply with requirements, and apply for benefits with the minimum possible burden. Documents that appear cluttered and dense create a negative reaction in the minds of our readers. We've heard many times from readers that when they get a dense, uninviting document from the government, they often put it in the "to be read later" pile, even though they know they should read it right away.

Document design is an important part of developing an effective document. Documents that are easy on the eye are far easier to understand than more traditional styles. You can use design elements to highlight important points and to ensure your user reads the most important parts of the document.

Even with regulations and the limits of publishing in the Code of Federal Regulations, you can replace blocks of text with headings, tables, and lists to create more white space. Short sentences and sections will also break up a regulation into visually manageable chunks. You will help your audience by making the main points readily apparent and grouping related items together. The easier it is for your audience to get through the regulation, the more likely it is they will comply with its requirements.

Here are a few brief guidelines for good document design:

- Have five or six sections on each printed page (about two on each typewritten page)

- Use lists and tables often, but don't overuse them and don't have lists within lists

- Use ragged right margins where possible, rather than fully justifying your text

Sources
- Schriver, Karen, *Dynamics in Document Design: Creating Text for Readers*, 1996, John Wiley and Sons, Hoboken, NJ.

IV. Write for the web

This section refers to the audience as users since that is a more common term in the web community. To effectively communicate with your web users, you must use plain-language techniques to write web content. This section will explain the differences between print and web writing and how to create sites that work for your users.

a. How do people use the web?

People use the internet to easily find, understand, and use information to complete a task. Unlike print media, people do not read entire web pages. They scan instead. Nielsen and Morkes, in a famous 1997 study, found that 79 percent of their test users always scanned any new page they came across; only 16 percent read word-by-word.

Even with more people using the web, the percent of content that is read on a website has not increased by much. Here are some facts to consider when writing web content:

- In a 2008 study, based on analysis of 45,237 page views, Nielsen found that web users only read about 18% of what's one page.

- As the number of words on a page goes up, the percentage read goes down.

- To get people to read half your words, you must limit your page to 110 words or fewer.

What do web users look at?

Since we know web users scan web pages, we need to learn what they look at.

Users often scan pages in an F pattern focusing on the top left side of the page, headings, and the first few words of a sentence or bulleted list. On average, users only read the first two words on each line. Also, users can decide in as little as five seconds whether your site is useful to them.

Here is an image of one of the eye tracking pages. The red shows where the user looked the most:

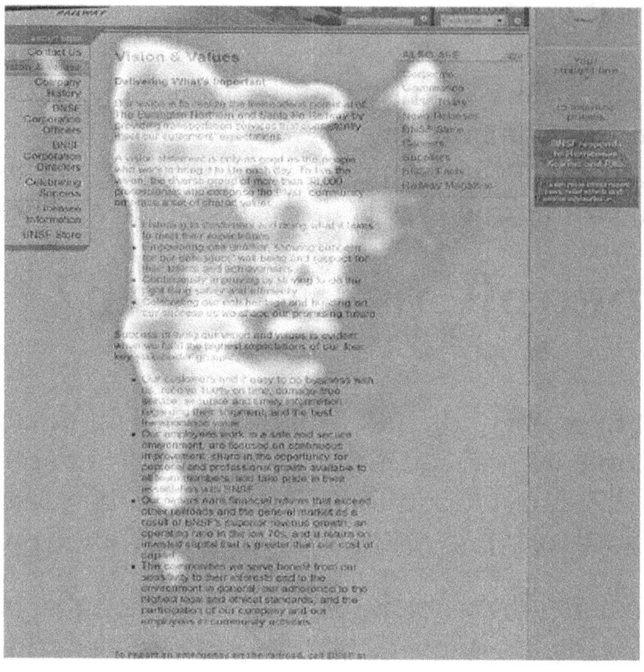

Sources

- www.useit.com/alertbox/percent-text-read.html
- www.customercarewords.com/what-it-is.html
- *Eyetracking Web Usability*, New Riders Press, December 14, 2009
- www.uie.com/articles/five_second_test/

b. Write for your users

Think about how well your website allows customers to get something done.

- Customers come to your site to perform a task.

- They come because they expect to get self-service.

People come to your website with a specific task in mind. If your website doesn't help them complete that task, they'll leave.

You need to identify the mission — the purpose — of your website, to help you clarify the top task your website should help people accomplish.

c. Identify your users and their top tasks

In order to write for your users, you need to know who they are! Here are some general tips to help you identify your users:

- Listen to user questions — what do your visitors ask when they send you an email or call your office?

- Talk to users and ask them what they want.

- Analyze your web metrics to figure out what people are looking for on your website:

- What are your most-visited pages and where do people spend the most time?

- What top search phrases do people use?

There are many techniques to help you learn about your users. For details and best practices visit www.usability.gov.

Source
- www.customercarewords.com/how-it-works.html

d. Write web content

After identifying your users and their top tasks, it is time to actually write web content. If you think it would be easy to just duplicate information you've written for print documents, you are wrong. While the information is helpful, it's not in the right format for the web. Remember, people scan web pages and only read about 18 percent of what's on the page! This means you need to cut whatever you have in print form by 50 percent!

Good web content uses:

- **The inverted pyramid style**. Begin with the shortest and clearest statement you can make about your topic. Put the most important information at the top and the background at the bottom.

- **Chunked content**. Don't try to pack everything into long paragraphs. Split topics up into logical sections separated by informative headings.

- **Only necessary information:** Use only the information your users need to achieve their tops tasks. Omit unnecessary information.

Remember:

Your content is **NOT** clear unless your users can:

- Find what they need

- Understand what they find

- Use what they find to meet their needs

Source

- Nielsen, Jakob, *Designing Web Usability: The Practice of Simplicity* (and other works), 1999, New Riders Publishing, Indianapolis.
- McGovern, Gerry, Killer Web Content: Make the Sale, Deliver the Service, Build the Brand (and other works), 2006, A&C Black.
- Redish, Janice, *Writing Web Content that Works*, 2007, Morgan Kaufmann Publishers, San Francisco.

e. Repurpose print material for the web

Don't cut and paste the text of print documents to create web content. People are more likely to leave your webpage, potentially costing you time and money, because they will not take the time to find what they are looking for.

Print writing is different from web writing. Print is very linear and narrative driven. In print, you can go into great detail about mundane things like eating breakfast. If you are a great writer, that can be an interesting story. But, those interesting stories don't work on the web. Instead they slow down web users who are trying to accomplish a task.

Jakob Nielsen (useit.com) explains that "Web users want *actionable* content; they don't want to fritter away their time on (otherwise enjoyable) stories that are tangential to their current goals."

Because the web is "action-oriented," you need to repurpose your print document.

Pick out necessary information in your print document that will help your web users and create a new web page.

- Keep the most important and clear message at the top of the web page

- Chunk your content into logical sections

- Use headings to help users navigate the content

- Highlight key facts in a bulleted list

- Explain complex instructions in a visually appealing If/Then table.

Source
- www.useit.com/alertbox/print-vs-online-content.html

f. Avoid PDF overload

Posting PDF versions (PDFs) of original documents on your site would seem to be an obvious alternative to re-writing your content in web-format. Unfortunately, this would work against your goal of retaining users. Posting too many PDF documents on your website can work against you. The Nielsen group has done multiple studies on PDFs and has consistently found that users hate them and try to avoid reading PDFs at all costs.

PDF files:

- Are slow to open and can sometimes crash a computer if they are too large

- Are difficult for some screen users to read

- Can make a user lose the website if they open in the same window

If you need to post a PDF use a gateway page — a web page that includes information about the PDF, including.

- What it's about

- How large the file is

- Who might find the information helpful

Remember to follow 508-compliance guidelines when using PDFs. See www.section508.gov for more information on 508-compliance.

Source:
- www.useit.com/alertbox/20030714.html

g. Use plain-language techniques on the web

We discussed plain-language techniques early in the guidelines. These techniques apply to web writing as well. Please refer to the specific section in the table of contents.

When writing web content

USE:

- Logical Organization

- Informative Headings

- Active Voice

- Use Pronouns

- Common Words

- Use lists and tables

AVOID:

- Jargon and legalese

- Hidden Verbs

- Passive Voice

- Long sentences or paragraphs

- Abbreviations

- Unnecessary Words

- Information the user doesn't want

h. Avoid meaningless formal language

Many government websites and letters contain meaningless formal language such as flowery welcome messages and "we hope you get a lot out of our program" messages. Using this type of language wastes space and your users' time. It conveys the impression that you are insincere. Don't waste your users' time. Instead, get directly to the point. Remember, time is money on the web. Keep your important information at the top of a web page. Don't bury it under fluff messages.

Here is a brief list of meaningless filler phrases:

- Thinking outside the box

- Value added

- Best practice

- For all intents and purposes

- Touch base

- Integrating quality solutions

- Promoting an informed and inclusive multicultural society

- Strategically engaging schools, community organizations, and so on . . .

Source
- Redish, Janice, *Writing Web Content that Works*, 2007, Morgan Kaufmann Publishers, San Francisco.
- www.contentini.com/writing-better-tips/

i. Write effective links

Links are about both content and navigation. Effective link names are key to satisfying your customers. The Eyetracking Studies showed links written in plain-language were the most effective. Plain-language links are written clearly so that the user understands exactly where the link will take them.

- Link names should be the same as the page name linked to.

- Don't use the full name of a document or program as a link name.

- Be as explicit as you can — too long is better than too short.

- Make the link meaningful. Don't use "click here" or "more."

- Don't embed links in text. It just invites people to leave your text!

- Add a short description when needed to clarify the link.

Remember, some of your users might be visually disabled. Do not use "Click Here" or "Click the green button" links. Make sure your links are accessible to all users. You want to use links that clearly explain the content of the page it links to. If your link says "Annual Reports," then destination page must be titled "Annual Reports."

Sources

- McGovern, Gerry, Killer Web Content: Make the Sale, Deliver the Service, Build the Brand (and other works), 2006, A&C Black.
- Nielsen, Jakob, *Designing Web Usability: The Practice of Simplicity* (and other works), 1999, New Riders Publishing, Indianapolis.
- www.useit.com/alertbox/nanocontent.html

V. Test

Testing your documents should be an integral part of your plain-language planning and writing process, not something you do after the fact to see if your document (or your website) is a suc[of people.

The information gained in testing can save time in answering questions about your document later. Although we refer to "documents" in this section, use these same techniques to test individual web pages or complete websites. In fact, we recommend testing websites, documents, brochures, applications, mobile websites, videos, social media, and public affairs messages.

When should I start testing?

Start as soon as you have enough material to test. Don't wait until your website has been coded or your document is complete. You can test your new material using a Word or PowerPoint document; you can test a large website or document in sections. You can also test existing websites and documents.

Test as early as you can in the project, whether you're creating something new or making revisions. Test, make corrections based on feedback, and test again. Plan to test at least twice. This process of testing, revising, and re-testing is called "iteration." Iteration is part of what makes usability testing so effective.

What types of testing are available?

You can use several techniques to help you improve your document so that the final version will be successful:

- **Paraphrase Testing**: individual interviews, best for short documents, short web pages, and to test the questions on a survey

- **Usability Testing**: individual interviews, best for longer documents and web sites where finding the right information is important; also best for forms – see www.usability.gov

- **Controlled Comparative Studies**: large scale studies where you don't meet the people but you collect statistics on responses; use paraphrase testing and usability testing on a smaller scale first

Focus groups are discussions in which you learn about users' attitudes and expectations more than about whether they can find and understand information. Therefore, they are more relevant to understanding your audience before you write than to testing. For more on focus groups, see www.usability.gov/methods/analyze_current/learn/focus.html.

a. Paraphrase Testing

One-on-one paraphrase testing sessions with users work best for short documents, short web pages, and when testing the questions on a survey.

Paraphrase testing will tell you what a reader thinks a document means and will help you know if the reader is interpreting your message as you intended. (See VBA testing success)

Try to conduct 6 to 9 interviews on each document.

Ask the participant to read to a specific stopping point, known as a cue. Each time the participant reaches a cue, ask the participant to tell you in his or her own words what that section means. Take notes, writing down the participant's explanation in the participant's words. Do not correct the participant. When you review your notes later, wherever participants misunderstood the message, the document has a problem that you should fix.

Ask additional, open-ended questions.

- What would you do if you got this document?

- What do you think the writer was trying to do with this document?

- Thinking of other people you know who might get this document:

- What about the document might work well for them?

- What about the document might cause them problems?

This last question is important because sometimes people are more comfortable telling you what they think others might find confusing, rather than admitting that they don't understand something themselves.

Don't ask yes/no questions.

You won't get much usable information from that type of question.

With only 6 to 9 participants, paraphrase testing will not take a lot of time, and the time invested is worth it. Taking the time to test your document and change it based on what you learn may save you hundreds of hours later answering questions from your users or producing a second document clarifying the first one.

For longer documents where finding information is also important do usability testing. Usability testing is the best technique for booklets, regulations, and web sites. With usability testing, you test the document as a whole, not just individual paragraphs.

b. Usability Testing

One-on-one usability testing sessions with users work best when the participant actually uses the document to find and understand information.

Usability testing is the best technique for documents where people have to find the information before understanding it.   (See National Cancer Institute testing success)

When should I test?

You can conduct usability testing at any time that you have a draft. After you make changes based on the first round of usability testing, you can conduct a second round to see if your changes solved the problems you found without introducing new problems.

Who should I test?

You need to find three people to test your website or document.

Identify who your intended readers are. For example, individuals searching for medical information; taxpayers and tax professionals looking for forms; travelers wanting a passport.

Develop simple criteria and find three people who match them. For example, for travelers, the criteria might be: Adult U.S. citizens who haven't applied for or renewed a passport lately. The criteria don't need to be complicated.

Using your network of colleagues, friends, and family, find three people who, more or less, meet the criteria and will give you an hour of their time. Don't use members of your own team, but employees from a different team down the hall may be fine.

You're not required to get any special permission to do a usability test with only three people. Set aside a morning to conduct your test, and give each of the volunteers an appointment, one hour apart from each other.

What happens in a typical session?

A typical usability test session lasts about one hour with these parts:

- **Introduction.** You make the participant comfortable, explain what will happen, and ask a few questions about the person to understand their relevant experience.

- **Scenarios.** You give the participant very short stories suggesting they have a need for specific information and then you watch and listen as they find that information and tell you what they understand from what they found.

  An example of a scenario for the FAA web site might be: *You have a private pilot's license and you just moved to a new city. Find out if you need to tell FAA about your new address. If you do, find out how to do that.*

  You can also ask participants for their own scenarios. What would they come to the document you are testing to find out? Then watch and listen as they look for and try to understand the information.

  Typically, you ask people to "think aloud" as they work so you hear their words for what they are looking for and you hear how they understand what they find.

- **Debriefing.** At the end, you can ask neutral questions about the experience and follow up about any specific words or phrases.

What variations are there?

Variations on the one-on-one usability test:

- **Two people working together** (co-discovery). Their discussion is an easy form of think aloud.

- **Several people working independently** at the same time followed by a group discussion. This speeds up the time you spend in usability test sessions, but it only works if you have several usability test note-takers so you have someone watching and listening to each participant before you bring all the participants together for the discussion.

- **Comparative usability tests.** You can include different versions of your document. Because you have a small number of people, it is best to have each person work with both versions. You have to alternate which version people start with.

- **Remote moderated usability testing.** With web-based tools, you do not have to be in the same place as the participant. These tools allow you to draw participants from a wide geographic range without travel costs.

- **Remote unmoderated usability testing.** You can have large numbers of people participate through remote testing tools. (For federal agencies, this may require clearance through OMB.)

Where can I learn more?

Almost anyone can conduct a simple usability test and fix problems that you see the volunteers encounter. Use these resources to help learn how.

Books
Barnum, Carol. *Usability Testing Essentials: Ready, Set... Test!*, Morgan-Kaufmann/Elsevier, 2011.

Chisnell, Dana, and Rubin, Jeff. *The Handbook of Usability Testing, 2nd edition* (http://www.wiley.com/WileyCDA/WileyTitle/productCd-0470185481,descCd-DOWNLOAD.html)

Krug, Steve. *Rocket Surgery Made Easy (http://www.sensible.com/rocketsurgery/index.html)*

Courses
Web Manager University (WMU) offers webinars, seminars, and one- and two-day courses in usability topics.

"Conducting Usability Testing in the Wild" presented by Dana Chisnell (free archived WMU webinar)

Conferences
Usability Professionals' Association Annual Conference

Nielsen Norman Group conferences

User Interface Engineering holds an annual conference and training events

Additional resources:
Webcontent.gov

Usability.gov

Usability Professionals Association has local chapters which offer training and networking events

c. Controlled Comparative Studies

Collect quantitative data on how well the general public uses your final document.

Controlled comparative studies can be done in several different ways, but they all have similar characteristics. Before you do a controlled study, you should know what results you will consider a success. For instance:

- Do you want more calls regarding a certain program?

- Do you want fewer calls asking for clarification?

- Do you want more people to return an application or a payment?

- Do you want fewer errors on forms people fill out?

Having answers to these questions will help you determine whether your document is successful. Controlled comparative studies are often called A/B testing. You have two (or more versions) of your page – A, B, etc.

Websites and web pages.

Set your web server to send each on a specific schedule (every other call to the page, or one today and the other tomorrow, or one for a certain longer period and the other for the next equal period). Just be sure you can track whatever measure you want by which version the web site visitor saw.

Paper documents.

Send a small test group of people the new version of your document. Let's say you're sending the new version to 700 people. You should also send 700 people, your control group, the old document. Track the responses to all 1400 documents and compare the results. Note that it is much easier to test results when people return a written response than when you try to track the number of phone calls you receive. (If you have a statistician or actuarial staff, they can tell you how many people you should use to make your study scientifically valid. If your agency doesn't have an expert on staff to help you, statistics books will give you a formula to determine a good sample size for your study.)

There are numerous other ways of collecting quantitative data. For instance, you can record what percentage of your "before" letters generates correct responses compared to your "after letters," or what percentage of each letter results in your customer calling you asking for an explanation.

Before you do a controlled comparative study, you should do paraphrase testing or usability testing and change you document based on what you learn in these smaller scale studies. Controlled comparative studies (especially for paper documents) are best near the end of the process. This is because controlled testing will tell you if the new document is a success, but it won't tell you why it is or isn't a success.

d. Testing Successes

We offer two examples of federal agency success with testing. If you have other examples, please let us know.

1. Paraphrase Testing from the Veterans Benefits Administration

The information was so general that it would have generated calls:
Veterans Benefits Administration tested a letter in which users appeared to understand every word. However, when asked what they would do if they got this letter, most people said they would call VBA's toll-free number.

The letter was about a replacement check sent because the original check was out of date. The letter said, "You will receive the new check shortly." Readers indicated that they would call if they didn't receive the check at the same time as the letter. Changing the sentence to show an approximate date they would receive the check eliminated countless phone calls.

A "term of art" that VBA thought veterans understand would have caused readers to take the wrong action:
When testing a multi-use letter, some readers were confused by the term "service-connected disability." To VBA it means that a veteran has a disability that can be traced back to time in military service." Protocol tests showed that one veteran thought it meant a disability that happened at work. Another thought it meant you had to be injured while in the military, but not necessarily while on duty. Another thought you had to have gotten the disability during combat for it to be considered service-connected.

When each reader was asked a general question about understanding the letter, they all said that it was clear. Yet several would have done something other than what VBA wanted because they had a different definition of "service-connected." To solve this problem, VBA explained the phrase so that everyone was working from the same definition.

Adding a word to make something more legally sufficient would have caused readers to give incorrect information:
A team working on a form wanted to use the question, "When were you last (gainfully) employed?" They felt that the term "gainfully employed" would gather more legally sufficient and accurate information than just the word "employed."

Testing showed that readers used at least three different definitions of "gainful" employment:

- Any job
- A job that provides benefits or where you can put money away
- A job that keeps you above poverty level

In fact, research showed that different government agencies may have different definitions of "gainful." But, more importantly, because each reader had a different definition of the word, the agency would have gotten less accurate information if the word had been in the document.

Remember, the goal of paraphrase testing is to ensure that your audience understands your document, and therefore, won't have to call you for an explanation. Although this technique is very valuable, it probably isn't worth the time to test documents that go to only one or a very few people.

2. Usability Testing from the National Cancer Institute

The information was good, but the title confused people.

A team at the National Cancer Institute tested a brochure on skin cancer prevention. They wanted to make sure that the information, title, and design images worked together well. One of the important messages was that even people with dark skin can get skin cancer. People understood the information in the brochure, but said that the title, "People of Color Get Skin Cancer, Too," made them think it was only for African-Americans.

The team changed the title to "Anyone Can Get Skin Cancer" (along with some other changes from the usability test recommendations) and tested it again. This time, when people were asked who the information in the brochure was for, they correctly identified many different people. More importantly, they all said that the information was "for them," too.

The team included both plain language experts and medical subject matter experts. This case study illustrates three points:

- Plain language experts test their work.

- Even a small change can make a big difference in the success of the project.

Retesting after you make a change is important. The second test may validate your decisions; it may also suggest additional changes.